The Way It Was
The North Dakota Frontier Experience
Book Five: Native People

Published in the Series

The Way It Was:
The North Dakota Frontier Experience

Book One: The Sod-busters, 1996

Book Two: Norwegian Homesteaders, 1998

Book Three: The Cowboys & Ranchers, 1999

Book Four: Germans from Russia Settlers, 1999

Book Five: Native People, 2002

Coming in 2002

Book Six: The Townspeople

The Way It Was

*The North Dakota Frontier Experience
Book Five:*

Native People

Everett C. Albers and D. Jerome Tweton, Editors

THE GRASS ROOTS PRESS
Fessenden, North Dakota 58438
2002

This book is dedicated to the memory of the first peoples of North Dakota. *Mitakuye Oyasin* — "We are all relatives."

Editors: *D. Jerome Tweton and Everett C. Albers*
Designer: *Otto Design of Bismarck, ND*

© 2002 by The Grass Roots Press

PO Box 407
Fessenden, North Dakota 58438-0407

Copyright is claimed in the Prefaces; Introductions to the Interviews collected by the Works Progress Administration in cooperation with the State Historical Society of North Dakota; Index; and Editing of the original Interviews which are in the public domain. All rights reserved to the material for which copyright is claimed.

Published by The Grass Roots Press

Printed in Canada

10 9 8 7 6 5 4 3 2 1

First Edition

International Standard Book Number: 0-9650778-5-3 (Book 5)
International Standard Book Number: 0-9650778-1-0 (6 Volume Set)

Library of Congress Catalog Card Number: 95095347

Table of Contents

Table of Contents

Illustrations		ii-iii
Acknowledgments		iv
Native People: Differences and Similarities	D. Jerome Tweton	v-ix
Turning Eagles into Crows	Everett C. Albers	x-xxii
A Witness to Sitting Bull's Death	James All Yellow	1-3
Horse Raiding and Buffalo Hunting	Eugene Bear Heart	4-6
When Worlds Collide	Frank Bull Bear	7-12
Life Around Fort Totten	Robert Charbonneau	13-19
Hunting, Trapping, and the Circus, Too	Michael Davis	20-26
Trouble with the Crow	Eagle Staff	27-28
A Lakota Childhood	Follows the Road	29-30
A Seven-Year Journey and the Life After	Zilda and Patrick Gunville	31-38
A Family of Yanktonai Medicine Men	Martin Iron Bull	39-41
Over One Hundred Years on the Plains	Louis Lafontaine	42-44
Adjustment to the Reservation	Robert Little Bird	45-47
Hunting Buffalo and Fighting Blackfeet	Many Horses	48-50
Farming near Pembina and in the Turtle Mountains	Ouiskin and Wanapi Rising Sun and Lone Child	51-54
Mandan and Hidatsa Ways	Sitting Crow	55-58
	Poor Wolf	58-60
On Lakota Life	Skylark Fly (Charles Ramsey)	61-66
Before the Reservation: Chippewa Ways	Standing Chief	67-73
The Killing of Sitting Bull	Swift Hawk	74-76
Fighting Custer, Fleeing to Canada	Two Bulls	77-79
Childhood, Marriage, A Deadly Fire, and an Eclipse of the Sun	Pretty Shawl	80-82
Index		83-84
About the Editors		85

Illustrations

Illustrations

Descendants of the Original Inhabitants of Dakota Territory Hand tinted by Thelma and Sylvia Wick of Fred Hultstrand's studio staff	Fred Hultstrand History in Pictures Collection, North Dakota Institute for Regional Studies-North Dakota State University, Fargo (*Hultstrand*) http://memory.loc.gov/ammem/award97/ndfahtml/ngphome.html	front cover
Maps of Movement of Native Peoples into North Dakota Geographical Region	created by Everett C. Albers	vi
Map of Indian Land Cessions in North Dakota	from Mary Jane Schneider, North Dakota's Indian Heritage (Grand Forks, ND: The University of North Dakota Press, 1990)	xiii
Polygala senega	from C.F. Millspaugh, American Medicinal Plants (New York: Dover Publications, 1974) engraving of root (insert) from Harvey Wickes Felter, M.D., and John Uri Lloyd, Phr. M., Ph. D., King's American Dispensatory, 1898.	xvii
Sitting Bull (Tatanka Iyotake)	Undated, unattributed engraving of a drawing made from the 1882 photograph of Sitting Bull by R.L. Kelley, from the Collection of Everett C. Albers	xxi
Red Tomahawk, Photograph by Frank Fiske	State Historical Society of North Dakota *SHSND Fiske 6101*	2
North Dakota State Patrol Logo	North Dakota State Patrol	2
Bison Attack Indian Horses by George Catlin	©2002 www.arttoday.com	
A Little fresh meat for the Indians: taken before the opening of the Rosebud Reservation, near Winner, South Dakota, 1880.	*Hultstrand*	11
Painting in oil - Fort Totten, D.T., by Conger (1890), after sketch by Louis Voelkner (1867)	*SHSND 78.121*	14
Crow Warriors	©2002 www.arttoday.com	28

ii

Indians traveling from Pembina, North Dakota to Fort Totten, North Dakota: Gathering Senega Root or Snakeroot	*Hulstrand*	36
Beef Issue Standing Rock Reservation	*SHSND C0844*	46
Rising Sun and Simaquam his wife, Chippewa	*SHSND A6767*	52
Poor Wolf	*SHSND A0137-02*	60
Burial Scaffold, Huffman photo 1882	*SHSND 0119-07*	65
Traveling by Red River Cart	*Chester Fritz Library, Elwyn B. Robinson Department of Special Collections, University of North Dakota* *UND*	69
Chief Little Shell	*SHSND B0307*	73
Indian Policemen, Standing Rock Reservation, Ft. Yates, ND	*SHSND Fiske 0305*	75
Sitting Bull and Crazy Horse at the Little Big Horn by Amos Bad Heart Bull	*Reproduced from* A Pictographic History of the Oglala Sioux *by Amos Bad Heart Bull, text by Helen H. Blish, published by the University of Nebraska Press*	78
Oglala Sioux Perform Dance with Horses by Kills Two	*from Hartley B. Alexander,* Sioux Indian Painting, *Volume I, Editions d'Art (Nice: C. Szwedzicki, 1938)*	81
Chief Two Bears ca 1877	*SHSND 0004-024*	82

Acknowledgments

Acknowledgments

The editors thank the staff of the State Historical Society of North Dakota, especially those in the Society's library and archives, which house the 5,000 WPA interviews and North Dakota photographs. They are always helpful in a cheerful way. John Bye of the Institute for Regional Studies at North Dakota State University, as usual, gave us his time and support. Illustrations and photographs which are used in this volume are credited throughout the book and on pages ii-iii.

About the Selection and Editing

Of the 5,000 pioneer interviews that the WPA conducted in North Dakota, very few involved Native People. Of those, with the exception of one Yankton and one Yanktonai, all were with Lakota and Chippewa people. For whatever reason, no interviewer set foot on the Fort Berthold Reservation of the Three Tribes; thus, no interview with Mandan, Hidatsa, or Arikara (Sanish) exists in the WPA files. Only an interview with a reservation missionary tells us anything about Mandan and Hidatsa ways. In spite of those limitations, the editors have selected nineteen interviews which provide the reader with rare glimpses into the lives of Native People.

In the editing, those interviews that were originally written in the third person have been recast to the first-person. We have made routine editorial changes to clarify sentences and punctuation.

D. Jerome Tweton

Native People: Differences and Similarities

D. Jerome Tweton

"We Indian people, like the winged ones, are all different, but like the winged ones, we are all alike."

"One of the most common errors is that all Indians are one people, of one language and of similar habits all over the continent. This is far from true." — Melvin Gilmore

IN HIS PIONEERING STUDY OF NORTHERN PLAINS Native People, *Prairie Smoke* (1929), ethnobotanist Melvin Gilmore makes the following point: "There are many false notions and erroneous ideas about Indians current everywhere. Our people (whites) should be better informed.... One of the most common errors is that all Indians are one people, of one language and of similar habits all over the continent. This is far from true." His observation was on target, as evidenced by the Native People who are an intrinsic part of North Dakota's story. Differences exist among the people, but, at the same time striking similarities characterize those same people.

A story that Hidatsa grandmothers told to the children goes a long way toward explaining the nature of Indian ways:

> Look at the eagle. It soars through the air and swoops down with a terrible noise. And it has feathers. Look at the duck. It

Native People: Differences and Similarities

flies through the air and swims on the water and it quacks. And it has feathers. Look at the owl. It sits in the tree and looks wise and hoots. And it has feathers. Look at the sparrow. It flits around and chirps. And it has feathers. We Indian people, like the winged ones, are all different, but like the winged ones, we are all alike.

The point is beautifully made: Native People have much in common, but they have differences as well.

Five distinct different groups of Indian people eventually became a part of North Dakota's history: the Mandan, the Hidatsa, the Sanish (Arikara), the Chippewa (Ojibwa), and the Great Sioux Nation (Lakota, Nakota, Dakota). These peoples were quite different from one another in several ways.

First, they traveled different paths to the region. The Mandan, followed by the Sanish, made their way up the Missouri River, perhaps as early as the fifteenth century. A bit later the Hidatsa moved from the Devils Lake area to the Missouri Valley. The Chippewa, closely allied with the French, followed the westward movement of the fur trade from the St. Lawrence Valley in Canada along the shores of Lake Superior and into Minnesota, where most remained. Two bands, however, followed the trade to Pembina and became the Plains (Turtle Mountain) Chippewa.

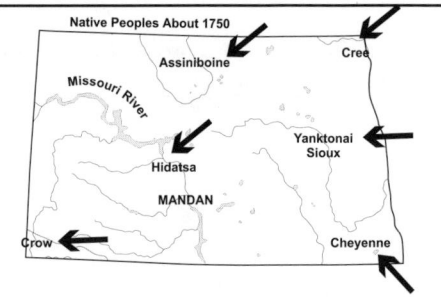

Arrows show probable movement into state. The Crow & Cheyenne passed through the lower part of what is now North Dakota.

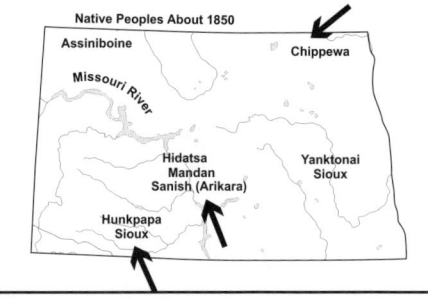

The Siouan people, according to archaeologists, originated in the East, perhaps North Carolina, followed the Ohio Valley westward, and ended up in Wisconsin and Minnesota. Three distinct

D. Jerome Tweton

divisions of the Great Sioux Nation had emerged. The Dakota, also referred to as the Santee, remained in Minnesota along the Mississippi and Minnesota rivers. Two Dakota bands, the Wahpeton and Sisseton, moved toward the West and hunted the prairies of eastern North and South Dakota. The Yankton/Yanktonai, also referred to as the Nakota, remained mostly in the valley of the James River. The Lakota, sometimes called the Tetons, was the largest and most powerful of the Sioux Nation and came to control the Plains from Kansas into Canada and westward into Wyoming and Montana. The Black Hills became especially important to them. Dakota's Native People came from different places to a uniquely different place.

Second, they did not always get along together. The Chippewa, armed with French guns, drove the Nakota and Lakota onto the Plains; the Lakota pushed the Sanish northward along the Missouri. The interviews in this book reflect the animosity between the Chippewa and the Siouan people. The conflict between the Sanish and the Lakota was long-standing.

Third, they pursued different ways of life. The Mandan, the Hidatsa, and eventually the Sanish settled down on the banks of the Missouri River to become successful farmers who lived in permanent villages. The Chippewa blended trading with hunting, although some farmed. The Nakota economy was mixed: agriculture and hunting. The Lakota, however, were hunters, first and foremost.

Fourth, the Native People who moved onto present-day North Dakota's plains and prairie spoke three distinctly different languages: the Sanish, Caddoan; the Chippewa, Algonquian; and the Mandan, Hidatsa, and the tribes of the Great Sioux Nation, Siouan. A Chippewa could communicate with a Sanish only by sign language.

Yet, in spite of the major differences, similarities stand out. First, they all lived close to nature and Mother Earth, which they treated with great reverence. Creation accounts most often refer to coming from the womb of Mother Earth. They were one with nature for power and sustenance which explains their great respect for the earth and its creatures.

Second, the Native People depended upon the buffalo for food, shelter, tools, sacred gifts, warm clothing, and bedding. This was, of

Native People: Differences and Similarities

course, truer for the Lakota whose economy was based totally on hunting. Yet, the Chippewa, too, as the Gunville interview emphasizes, went on extended hunts into Montana. The Mandan, Hidatsa, and Sanish, known primarily as agriculturalist, conducted well-planned, seasonal buffalo hunts.

Third, kinship and family were all important to the Native People. Society was organized along family lines. A person was born into a clan or band, an extended family. This kinship meant that no one was alone, that everyone was cared for. Grandparents were given special respect as those who provided knowledge and wisdom.

Fourth, spirituality was central to everyone's life. To the Native People, a creator, whether referred to as the Great Spirit or the Great Mystery, controlled the universe. Ceremonies differed from group to group — Lakota, Sun Dance; Mandan, *Okipa*; Hidatsa, *Naxpike*; Chippewa, *Midewiwan*; but the reasons or results were the same: to renew sacred beliefs, put the universe in balance, and insure the protection of the spirits for the people.

Fifth, oral tradition kept the past alive. Each band or family had someone who was responsible for passing on the traditions and stories of their people. Grandparents often took on the roles of record keepers. How else would, as illustrated by several of the interviews, one know in detail what happened on a hunt when that person was a small child? The power of the oral tradition!

Sixth, all the Native People had to adjust to a new environment. When they moved from the woodlands of the East onto the Plains, life had to change. Food in the form of wild rice, fish, and forest game were no longer available. The buffalo became the new source of food. And, since the buffalo roamed over a vast region, the people too, had to move with the buffalo. This meant for the Lakota and most of the other tribes that the moveable tipi replaced the permanent wigwam, that the all-important horse replaced the canoe, that breakable pottery gave way to skin pouches for cooking. The soft-soled moccasin, comfortable in the woods, was terribly uncomfortable on the sun-baked plains. So, hard-soled moccasins became common. Life on the plains was much more difficult than life in the woodlands.

D. Jerome Tweton

Seventh, the coming of white people forever changed the lives of all Native People. Fur traders brought with them the devastating disease of smallpox which ravaged Indian populations. The 1781 epidemic killed upwards to 4,000 Mandan, and the plague of 1837 left 125 Mandan alive. Traders also introduced alcohol to the Native People with, in many cases, disastrous consequences. Pembina fur trader Alexander Henry believed that white traders "have destroyed both mind and body with . . . RUM."

The westward march of white settlers and their demand for land, of course, led to conflict on the plains. The army with its chain of protective forts led the way for white settlement. The ultimate result was the reservation and the restriction of the Native People to those, often too small, reserves. Government policy attempted to turn hunters into farmers, to change Native People into white people. Toward that end Indian ways—ceremonies, religion, long hair, language — were banned. As the interviews in this book illustrate, the adjustment to the reservation was severe. The old life, the free life, was forever gone for all Native People.

The Hidatsa grandmother captured the heart of the matter when she concluded her story: "We Indian people, like the winged ones, are all different, but like the winged ones, we are all alike."

Turning Eagles into Crows

Everett C. Albers

"If the Great Spirit had desired me to be a white man he would have made me so in the first place. . . . It is not necessary for eagles to be crows." —
attributed to Sitting Bull, *Tatanka Iyotake*, (about 1831-1890)

> *"In future your business dealings with the whites are going to be very hard, and it behooves you to learn well what you are taught here. But that is not all. We older people need you. In our dealings with the white men, we are just the same as blind men, because we do not understand them. We need you to help us understand what the white men are up to."* —
> **Sitting Bull to the young people of Standing Rock, 1880s**

WITH THE POSSIBLE EXCEPTION OF SACAGAWEA, Sitting Bull continues to be the most recognized human who ever lived in this place to people beyond what is now the state of North Dakota. The state citizens will soon send a statue of her with her infant son, Jean Baptiste Charbonneau, on her back to the National Statuary Hall in the U.S. Capitol. North Dakotans spell the Bird Woman's name Sakakawea. Among other tributes to her memory is the huge Lake Sakakawea behind Garrison Dam, which flooded much the Missouri River Valley in the 1950s, including the homes of the Hidatasa, Mandan, and Arikara living on the bottomlands on Fort Berthold. She

Everett C. Albers

has become a state and national heroine. Born a Shoshone, she is claimed by the North Dakota Hidatsa people with whom she was living when Lewis and Clark arrived in 1804. She almost certainly died in 1812 at Fort Manuel in what is now South Dakota.

More than sixty years after he was killed in his cabin just across the South Dakota border, North Dakotans, including many of the Native People, are not sure that Sitting Bull was a hero — or a particularly good man, for that matter. Up to his death in 1890, he had little good to say about the changes brought by white people. Unlike some of those from Standing Rock Reservation who were there that December when he was killed, Sitting Bull stubbornly held on to the old traditions, even when adapting to the disappearance of the buffalo and the white invasion became the only alternative to cultural — and, for the Hunkpapa spiritual leader — physical death.

The nineteen narratives in this book are told by Native People of this place who found a way to keep the best of their cultural heritage through very difficult times. Many of the stories are tinged with a poignant nostalgia for a more elemental relationship with this place, a time when they lived by hunting and gathering, when they lived in portable houses they could easily carry with them, when elders were respected and children learned what they needed to know without sitting at desks in a school.

The elders interviewed in the 1930s, some of whom spoke through interpreters, came to adulthood long before the white invasion forced Indians on the plains to set aside their traditional differences. They often spoke of tribes other than their own as enemies, the "others" from whom they stole horses, the enemies they killed and were killed by in conflicts that had been a way of life for generations. At the turn of the twenty-first century, few Native People in North Dakota speak with such frankness about tribal warfare. Eugene Bear Heart, who was about eighty years old when he was interviewed, recalled with pride killing and scalping eleven Crows — the entire band the group of young warriors he was with encountered — except for one who "was too fast and got away." Louis Lafontaine from the Turtle Mountain Reservation, well over one hundred years old when he told his story in the 1930s, begins by recalling how his mother was murdered by marauding

Turning Eagles into Crows

Sioux. When Lafontaine tried to scalp the Sioux he had killed, including the one he thought had shot his mother, he was stopped by his father because the family had converted to Catholicism. The Lakota warrior Many Horses spoke of the constant danger of following the buffalo west from his home in what is now central North Dakota: ". . . one was apt to run into roving bands of Crow, Pawnee, and Blackfeet Indians." At the end of his story, Many Horses speaks of the change that took place in his lifetime, for he later met — in a peaceful, social setting — the same Blackfeet who were involved in the fight he had with them as a young man. Sitting Crow, born in 1861 at Like-A-Fishhook village where the Hidatsa, Mandan, and their old enemy, the Arikara, lived together after smallpox nearly wiped out what are now the Three Affiliated Tribes, recalled getting close enough to a Sioux who had stolen his people's horses to count coup on the thief, to strike him with a stick.

The way of life for the native people of North Dakota changed enormously in the short decades after the beginning of the war between the Sioux and the United States government following the flight of Dakota people from Minnesota after the Uprising in 1862 and its conclusion with the killing of Sitting Bull and the death of 300 Sioux — including many women and children — at Wounded Knee in 1890. When native elders recalled the 1880s fifty years later, they sometimes spoke with understandable resentment at their confinement to ever-dwindling reservations. Within two years, the home base of the Chippewa and the Métis at Turtle Mountain was reduced from an area thirty by thirty-three miles to six by twelve miles, two townships. Suddenly, hundreds of people who had called the area around the Turtle Mountains home found themselves landless. They journeyed to Montana and western Dakota Territory and north to Canada in search of land, for the buffalo were gone, game was scarce, and they were prohibited from practicing their traditional religion on the tiny reservation. Within a few short, tumultuous years, the native peoples of what became North Dakota in 1889 found themselves with a common enemy, the white invaders who demanded more and more of their homeland. Ravaged and decimated by the greatest scourge brought by the whites even before Lewis and Clark enjoyed their hospitality in

Everett C. Albers

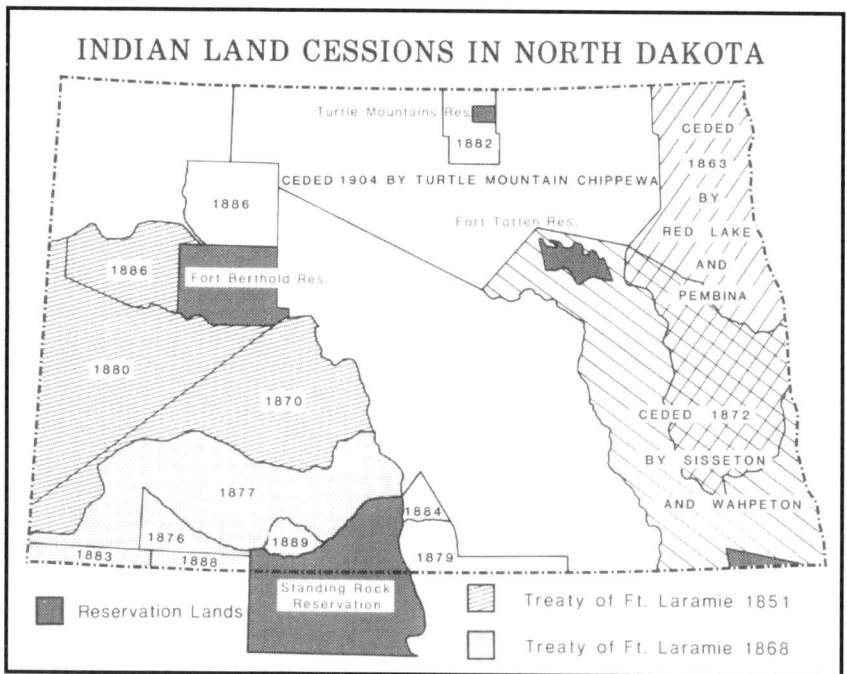

Reducing the Native People's Homeland

1804-1805, the village people of the Missouri River had moved northwesterly up the Missouri and eventually settled on a much smaller reservation around Fort Berthold. The Treaty of Fort Laramie in 1851 had recognized Lakota, Arikara, Mandan, and Hidatsa claims to all of present-day North Dakota lying west and south of the Missouri River. By the late 1880s, only the poor land south of the Cannonball River remained in Standing Rock Reservation, and Fort Berthold was reduced from what was over twelve million acres in 1851 to less than one million by the mid-1880s.

Those who survived the changes of 1862-1890 and lived to be interviewed by WPA workers in the 1930s were, for the most part, what Major James A. McLaughlin (1842-1923) called "Progressives," those who adapted to the white man's laws and demands. Called White Hair by some of the Indians, McLaughlin was the Indian agent who sent out reservation policemen to arrest Sitting Bull in December 1890. He first came to Dakota Territory in 1871 to serve as the Indian agent at Fort Totten, and he was there when Robert Charbonneau witnessed the killing of one of the participants in a mock battle on the Fourth of July. Married to a Sioux mixed-blood, McLaughlin learned the language and was instrumental in most of the changes in the lives of the Indians in the 1880s. He assumed responsibility for Standing Rock in 1881, and he quickly changed the judicial and educational system, including establishing day schools remembered with such bitterness by Frank Bull Bear who cried when McLaughlin's policemen forced him to go to school where the teacher cut his hair. As a special agent of the Office of Indian Affairs in 1901, he persuaded the people of Fort Berthold to sell much of their land east of the Missouri. In his long career among the native peoples of what became North Dakota, McLaughlin worked tirelessly to "civilize" them — to turn the hunters and warriors into farmers, or, as Sitting Bull put it, turn eagles into crows. Forcing the Indians to farm was difficult enough: as Robert Little Bird remembered, "My father did not like farming, so my mother and I did all of the work." When McLaughlin decided to make the Indians ranchers instead of farmers, he ran into another problem: Indian generosity, the "give-aways" so lamented by many government agents among Native People. James All Yellow, one of McLaughlin's Indian police, remembered that he had over one hundred horses and eighty cattle in the early 1900s. "I gave away many horses and cows to other Indians." Frank Bull Bear also was a successful rancher until about 1920, but like All Yellow and Little Bird, he was forced off the range by whites who bought or leased much of the land. Moreover, he gave too much away: "As was the custom when hungry, they [landless Indians] came to my house, and I killed a beef for them."

There were cultural impediments to becoming "civilized," to the Native People becoming competitive citizens of a capitalistic society. If they were to survive, they would have to be Christianized; they would have to give up their religion. On Standing Rock in 1890, it was the Ghost Dance, brought to the plains from Nevada where Wovoka had a vision of returning the country to the way it was before the white man came, that sent settlers hundreds of miles away scurrying for safety. They had no reason to worry. There were no Sioux on the warpath and no evidence that Sitting Bull's followers planned any kind of uprising. It is doubtful that Sitting Bull believed Wovoka's promise, but he allowed dancing in his camp on Standing Rock, across the present-day North Dakota/South Dakota border on the Grand River, because he thought it was a harmless diversion from the hard times they were living. He really did not think that the buffalo would return. On the other hand, he was not about ready to turn himself from an eagle into a crow for the white men.

Many recalled meeting Sitting Bull, including the Métis Robert Charbonneau, who was at Fort Totten when the infamous Hunkpapa leader visited in the 1880s. In many ways, Charbonneau did not consider himself Indian. He was a Christian who admired the work of Father Jerome among the natives suffering from a smallpox epidemic. But the "Indians" were primitives who held a Sun Dance during the epidemic in the hope that it would stop the scourge. Moreover, he was gainfully employed as a carrier of freight and mail, and he had an established home. That he was, as his mother claimed, the grandson of Sacagawea is contradicted by the historical record. Charbonneau had little good to say of Sitting Bull: "I do not know why Sitting Bull came to the fort; the officers feared to have him mingling with Indians on the reservation as he never failed to stir up trouble, the Indians being very restless after one of his visits. My memory of Sitting Bull is a homely, stupid, Sioux Indian, but I guess that Sitting Bull was smarter than he looked."

Chippewa Michael Davis recalled seeing Sitting Bull in Canada, near Fort Assiniboine in 1878. According to Davis, Sitting Bull was invited by a Canadian captain to settle down on a reservation. Sitting Bull refused the offer of help. He wanted to be alone. Davis quotes Sitting Bull as saying, "When I was home in the Black Hills, I did not quit until my arm got tired of hitting the white men."

Three of those included in this volume were in Fort Yates when Sitting Bull was killed: James All Yellow, an Indian policeman who went to Sitting Bull's camp; Skylark Fly (Charles Ramsey), who was employed repairing harnesses at Fort Yates and who prepared the dead policemen for burial when they were brought in; and Swift Hawk, who was a policeman wounded in the attempted arrest of Sitting Bull. Swift Hawk says that "Most of these [stories about ghost dance activities in Sitting Bull's camp] were exaggerated or untrue. Mc Laughlin sent

Turning Eagles into Crows

Indian policemen out to Sitting Bull, telling him to stop dancing. Sitting Bull sent back word that they were not doing any harm and would not stop." After the unexpected and unfortunate fight at Sitting Bull's camp, Swift Hawk says that "Feeling ran very high, and many Indians were very angry with the policemen. Policemen had to be very careful for many years after this as many of the Indians held this fight against them."

The descendants of Sitting Bull and those Indians who "were very angry with the policemen" were not interviewed by WPA workers. Even those who were disgruntled with the way whites changed their lives, like the school truant Frank Bull Bear who mananged to drop out of the white man's school, carefully distanced themselves from Sitting Bull: "The Indians around the Cannon Ball Agency were friendly to the white people. We took no part in the Sitting Bull trouble. We knew he was a trouble maker, and we had nothing to do with him or his Indians."

For whatever reason, the WPA project in North Dakota, so overwhelmingly successful in recording the stories of pioneer homesteaders in the 1930s, did precious little to tap the incredible resources available among the tribal elders of the state's reservation. In fact, no interviews were done on Fort Berthold, home of the Three Affiliated Tribes, but the WPA project officials did accept two narratives from missionary Charles L. Hall: one of the Mandan Sitting Crow and another of the Hidatsa Poor Wolf, who survived the smallpox epidemic that nearly wiped out his people in 1837 when he was seventeen and who lived to see the first automobiles on Fort Berthold. A man of deep spirituality, Poor Wolf received his name and learned that he would live long from a warrior whose life he saved from starvation by giving him a piece of buffalo meat on a hunt. The warrior had a vision following an eight-day Sun Dance. Poor Wolf once caught twelve eagles on a successful hunt, and his protectors kept him from harm, even though he failed to weep for the killed eagles.

What might have been learned from those who survived the cultural changes following the confinement to reservations is only hinted at in tidbits of oral tradition seldom shared outside the native elders' tribal circles. Skylark Fly gives detailed information about how to hunt the eagle and how to act in the sacred manner after killing among the most revered of creatures: "As the hunter twisted the eagle's neck to kill it, he said a prayer. He called the eagle his grandfather and asked to be forgiven for killing the eagle. He was very sorry and cried real tears. To kill an eagle and not ask its forgiveness would bring bad luck. The hunter might lose his best horse or some member of his family might die."

Often, we are left with hints of something of far greater consequence than what is said. Why, for example, did so many travel the land around the Red River in search of senega root (*Polygala senega*, snake root)? Zilda and Patrick Gunville earned fifteen to twenty cents a pound for the fruit of their long summer journeys digging the root. Still gathered — and even cultivated — at the turn of the twenty-first century, the perennial takes four years to mature, and thirty to forty roots are needed to make a pound. Known to white physicians since the late 1600s, the root was used by eastern tribes, including the Seneca, to treat snakebite. It continues to be used widely for respiratory diseases. At the turn of the last century, it was exported to Europe for fifty-five to sixty cents a pound, where it was used to treat rheumatism and typhoid, among other ailments. For a time, it was a primary ingredient in expectorant cough syrups, and in the 1950s senega root from Manitoba brought Native People there an income of about $150,000 annually.

Polygala senega

Chippewa people often wore the root as a charm or carried it as a talisman. The Chippewa brewed a tea from the root which they used to induce abortion. Among the effects of the drug in men is increased sexual desire, but there are painful side effects.

We have only glimpses of lifeways far different from what white culture wanted the Native People to adopt. As a girl, the Lakota Follows the Road (her name in itself suggestive of "following a different path") had two pets. One was a bear cub that she "gave to grandfather," that is, killed and returned to its creator when "it became rough and had to be shot." The other was a pet skunk — "I tied a string around its neck, and

Turning Eagles into Crows

we would go out in the hills. The skunk would catch grasshoppers and worms, and I thought that was lots of fun." Was the skunk de-scented? We don't know. Curiously, at the dawn of the new millennium in 2001, over a quarter-million Americans kept skunks as pets. There's an annual national skunk show as well.

Chippewa Michael Davis did not have a pet skunk; he trapped them, along with muskrats, minks, foxes, and coyotes to make a living. Davis remembered meeting Louis David Riel (1844-1885), the leader of the Red River Rebellion , the fight between the Métis and the Canadian government that Louis Lafountaine took part in 1885. Both Davis and Lafountaine first met Riel in Montana. Davis says that he was asked by Riel to "get a young girl to take a few drops of whiskey." Riel told Davis that "I have tried to get her to drink a little of it, but she won't do it." Davis says, "The girl was a daughter of my cousin. I said I could get her to do it. After coaxing her a little while, the girl took a few drops of the liquor. A couple of days later Riel and the girl were married. I thought that Riel must have put a love potion in the whiskey."

We know from the historical record that Riel married Marguerita Monet in Montana in 1881 and that he was in the Judith Basin of Montana teaching Indian children in a Jesuit mission school when Canadian Métis came to him and asked him for help, as reported by Louis Lafountaine. What we have from the WPA interviews is a first-hand account of how Riel met his wife from one of her relatives. What Davis doesn't tell us is what was in the love medicine, the ingredient that Riel wanted to disguise with whiskey — or why he chose liquor as the way to give the girl the potion. Time and again as we read the all-too-brief and too-few narratives, we wonder why the interviewer didn't ask a few questions when presented with these jewels from the oral treasury of the state's Native People in the 1930s.

For example, Pretty Shawl told the interviewer that she ". . . was married four times. We did not have any marriage ceremony. If a man and woman liked each other, they went to live in one of their parents' tipis, or the man would be given a tipi of his own by his parents. If they did not get along, they separated and lived with someone else. When they separated, the chldren were left to be taken care of by the grandparents." Why did she marry so often? Were some of her husbands killed in war, as were three of her eleven brothers? Or did she choose unwisely? Did she have any children of her own? She didn't offer any additional information, and the interviewer didn't ask.

Martin Iron Bull, who succeeded his grandfather, father, and older brother as the medicine man for his Yanktonai band, told the interviewer that his people lived an average of eighty to ninety years before the white man came. He suggests that the secret to a long life was a healthy diet ("dried meat, roots, and dried wild fruit" in the winter) and as little clothing as possible ("only moccasins, breech cloth, mittens, and a skin cap" and "on the coldest days a buffalo robe thrown over the shoulders"). Much is not said, of course, because the elder being interviewed assumed that everyone knew certain things: older people enjoyed enormous prestige and great respect — they had every reason to live.

"My mother lived to be over one hundred years old. She died twice," says the Lakota woman Follows the Road who was in her 60s when she was interviewed — among the youngest of all of those who tell their stories in the pages that follow. Her mother was left for dead in a tipi when the camp moved on when Follows the Road was a child. When her father came back four days later, he saw "someone sitting in front of the tipi." Thinking it was a ghost, he slowly circled the tipi from a safe distance until his wife yelled at him. He finally approached, and they were reunited. They pack up the tipi and return to camp. "Everyone thought she had died and came back to life again. I still believe this is what happened," says Follows the Road in conclusion.

Why was her mother left with the tipi instead of being buried or put on a scaffold? Were women not given the rites accorded warriors, as reported by so many of those interviewed? Did they leave her in an emergency, some kind of enemy attack? In the paragraph before the story about her mother, Follows the Road tells how her father's body was wrapped in buffalo hides and deerskins and placed on a scaffold beneath an American flag because he had worked for the military at Fort Yates. On one of the poles, they placed the bugle given to him by one of the soldiers. Her mother was left to the scavengers. Why?

We know from several of the narratives that, as Follows the Road says, "The boys did about as they pleased, but the girls had to do some

Turning Eagles into Crows

work." Many Horses says, "The boys did whatever they wanted to, but the girls had to help their mothers." In the Chippewa culture, boys and girls shared chores, according to sources like Standing Chief, who remembered loading meat onto the carts during buffalo hunts. Zilda Gunville remembered the boys attending Mother Genevieve's school being sent to build a house on her homestead and the girls helping her poison gophers. Ouiskin recalled that her brothers and fathers spaded and planted the garden that her mother and she and her sisters then tended. How much young women had to say about whom they married is not addressed directly. The Lakota Skylark Fly says that young men courted the girls they wanted by "giving presents to her and her family." He does say that "The father usually took his time in saying 'Yes' as the longer he put off giving his girl away the more presents he would get."

We do learn that the roles of men, women, and children changed in a very short time, and that the culture of the native people was transformed to one that led to shorter, unhappier lives for most of those who told their stories for the WPA project.

Even those who tried to adapt found themselves thwarted by government policy and the white settlers' hunger for their land. Michael Davis concludes that "The white people used the tax situation as a club over the Indians to make them get off the land and crowd together in the two townships set aside as a reservation." Davis's family had tried everything to make a living, including performing as Indian dancers for a traveling circus. They were stranded in Iowa without "a cent of the nine hundred dollars we had coming." The Indians tried farming, some with the most primitive of tools, as did Louis Lafountaine when he broke the sod with a hatchet. Successful ranchers like Robert Little Bird say they were forced off their land on Standing Rock when "the reservation was opened to white people in 1915." Concludes Little Bird, "After we sold or leased our land most of us sold our cattle and horses. We no longer did any work, and hard times came upon us." Many Horses concludes, "We had few laws, but the ones we did have were obeyed. I cannot understand the white man's law. They make laws and then break them and also taught the Indians how to break them."

Everett C. Albers

Sitting Bull tried to adapt as well, as best he could. He was making a living on the Grand River when McLaughlin's policemen came to arrest him in December 1890. He had traveled the United States and gone to Europe with Buffalo Bill Cody, who did, in fact, pay him. He brought home the money that he did not give away to white beggars, especially the children, he met on his tour with the Wild West Show (the poverty in the midst of ostentatious wealth was something that Sitting Bull could never understand). For all of his reluctance to follow the white man's path, Sitting Bull was a practical leader who saw what was coming. He tried his very best to help his people. Few white settlers or their descendants know about a speech he made at the invitation of the Reverend Mr. Jerome Hunt to students at a Catholic school on Standing Rock:

My dear grandchildren: All of your folks are my relatives, because I am a Sioux, and so are they. I was glad to hear that the Black Robe had given you this school where you can learn to read, write, and count the way white people do. You are also being taught a new religion. You are shown how the white men work and make things. You are living in a new path.

When I was your age, things were entirely different. I had no teachers but my parents and relatives. They are dead and gone now, and I am left alone. It will be the same with you. Your parents are aging and will die some day, leaving you alone.

**Sitting Bull
(Tatanka Iyotake)**

So it is for you to make something of yourselves, and this can only be done while you are young. In my early days I was eager to learn and to do things, and therefore I learned quickly, and that made it easier for my teachers. Now I often pick up papers and books which have all kinds of pictures and marks on them, but I cannot understand them as a white person does. They have a way of communicating by the use of written symbols and figures; but before they could do that, they had to have an understanding among themselves. You are learning that, and I was very much pleased to hear you reading.

Turning Eagles into Crows

In future your business dealings with the whites are going to be very hard, and it behooves you to learn well what you are taught here. But that is not all. We older people need you. In our dealings with the white men, we are just the same as blind men, because we do not understand them. We need you to help us understand what the white men are up to. My Grandchildren, be good. Try and make a mark for yourselves. Learn all you can.

With all my heart I thank my Black Robe friends for their goodness and kindness towards me.

They did learn, those descendants of those interviewed in the 1930s about the way it was for them as they grew up in the place they came to share with white settlers in North Dakota. But seventy years after they told their stories, seventy plus seventy years and more since they grew up in this place, we descendants of the white settlers they lived with have yet to learn from them all they could have taught us about how to live happier lives in this place we now share with those who followed their path.

We would do well to read their stories carefully and to ask their chidren's children about what we do not understand. For all that was done to turn the native people of this state from eagles into crows, they found a way to remain eagles. They can, perhaps, teach us how to soar. The Black Robes Sitting Bull thanked, the well-meaning James McLaughlin who tried to "civilize" the Indians in his charge, and the white settlers who homesteaded the lands they owned — all assumed that the Native People had to change to survive. That much is certain, for the buffalo were gone, and the whites were here to stay.

But more than a century later, we are just beginning to understand that those people our ancestors dismissed as uncivilized had valuable lessons to teach us about living in this place the Native People have called home so much longer than we have. They understood about some things that can be seen only in visions, about the relationship with the natural landscape and other living creatures who live here that our people had long forgotten. They knew it all the time: indeed, "we *are* all relatives" — the eagles and the crows — *Mitakuye Oyasin!*

James All Yellow

A Witness to Sitting Bull's Death

James All Yellow

*Red Tomahawk...
shot Sitting Bull in the head.*

All Yellow was born in 1865 near present-day Aberdeen, South Dakota. His father, a hunter and warrior, had been born in present-day Nebraska about 1842 and was described as "a friend of the white people." All Yellow tells about what a Lakota childhood was like and his role as an Indian policeman. He was present when Sitting Bull was killed and relates his version of that event.

DURING BOYHOOD, I SPENT MY TIME PLAYING with the other children. My father and grandfather made bows and arrows for me. With these, I hunted birds and small animals. When I was about nine years old, my grandfather gave me a pony. I was very proud of this little horse, because it could run so fast. I spent much time riding in the hills and racing with the other boys. In the wintertime I played drums that my father had made and had a sled and three dogs to pull it.

There were about one hundred ten Indians in our band. There were two chiefs, Ghost Bull and Left Hand. We all lived in tipis and moved from place to place, depending on food and the weather. In the winter we moved into the timber along some stream.

A Witness to Sitting Bull's Death

Sometimes many of the different tribes would get together for a visit, exchange of gifts, and powwows about the government. There were horse races and games. Many of the Indians played gambling games.

Our food was buffalo, deer, rabbits, coyotes, birds, wild fruit, onions, and turnips.

We did not have much sickness, and most of the Indians lived to be very old.

In every tipi there were many children, and, besides their parents, there would be one or two old Indians.

As a young man I was a hunter and a trapper. I killed many buffalo, deer, and coyotes; and I trapped fur-bearing animals and traded the furs for guns, blankets, and cloth.

Our tribe was friendly to the white people and did not take part in the raids against them. Some of the young men went on horse-stealing expeditions against the Crows in Montana. Sometimes they brought back horses, and sometimes they were never seen again.

When I was twenty-four, I moved to Fort Yates and joined the Indian police and was given a saddle, rifle, pistol, a uniform, ten dollars a month, and food.

As a policeman I searched Indian homes for guns, carried messages from Fort Yates to outlying Indian substations, and arrested many unruly Indians. I was with the police that went out to arrest Sitting Bull in 1890.

I and Red Tomahawk were sent out after the other Indian policemen had left Fort Yates. I caught up with them in camp on the Grand River. Red Tomahawk carried large squares of white cloth. The policemen tied the cloth around their necks so they could tell who were policemen in the dark.

Red Tomahawk
This photograph of the Indian policeman who killed Sitting Bull by Frank Fiske (SHSND Fiske 6101) was the model for the official logo of the North Dakota Highway Patrol (insert).

2

James All Yellow

We then set out for Sitting Bull's camp, which we reached early on the morning of December 15, 1890. Bullhead was a second lieutenant and in command. Bullhead sent some of the men to search the nearby cabins. Bullhead, Red Tomahawk, Shavehead, and a few more went to Sitting Bull's cabin. They went into the house, and, as Sitting Bull would not go peaceably, they were taking him by force. Sitting Bull's boy cried and yelled, before the policemen could stop him.

Just as the policemen were taking Sitting Bull outside, the Sitting Bull Indians came running. They had guns and were yelling. One of them shot at the policeman, and in a second the Indians were shooting, running, and yelling. Bullhead and Shavehead, who were holding Sitting Bull, both fell mortally wounded. Red Tomahawk was back of them and shot Sitting Bull in the head. Some of the policemen ran in the cabin and killed Sitting Bull's boy. The fighting lasted about one hour. The policemen took refuge in cabins; some had crawled into a woodpile, and some were in the woods. The soldiers arrived at this time. From the top of a hill they fired down into Sitting Bull's camp. This made some of the policemen very angry. Red Tomahawk ran out of one of the cabins, waving his gun, which had a white cloth tied to it. The soldiers then stopped firing and came down to the camp. The Sitting Bull warriors had left by this time, and the soldiers did not kill any of the women and children who were left in camp.

I helped bring back the dead and wounded to Fort Yates.

After leaving the police service in 1900, I moved to Big Lake, a church and government school nine miles south of Cannon Ball, North Dakota. There I built a log cabin on my wife's land. I raised cattle and horses, and at one time had over a hundred head of horses and eighty head of cattle. I gave away many horses and cows to the other Indians. When the reservation was opened to white people, I gradually lost my herds, and in 1918 I moved to Cannon Ball.

Horse Raiding and Buffalo Hunting

Horse Raiding and Buffalo Hunting

Eugene Bear Heart

Most of our horses were taken from the Crow Indians . . .

Bear Heart was born about 1857 while his Sioux camp of about a thousand people were on the hunt in Montana. More than likely a Lakota, Bear Heart describes his people's method of buffalo hunting and explains how his tribe got some of its horses — at the expense of the Crow.

I WAS ABOUT EIGHTEEN when I killed my first buffalo with a bow and arrow made by my father. About one hundred Indians went out on this hunt. Except for one or two rifles, we used bows and arrows. There were small herds of buffalo on the hills, but we did not kill any of these since we were looking for a large herd. A few hunters rode ahead to locate the buffalo. They located a large herd about six miles from camp. We then separated into three groups. One group rode on each side of the herd, and a smaller group came up from the rear to kill wounded buffalo.

We rode on small ponies, and we were trained to run alongside the buffalo. When the signal was given, we dashed around a hill. The buffalo looked up and then started to move, not very fast, but as we came up closer, they started to run.

My pony ran up to the buffalo, but in the excitement I couldn't get my bow ready, and I dropped my arrow. My father dropped this buffalo for me. I went after another. This time I managed to shoot an arrow into the side of the buffalo but missed the heart. I shot two more arrows into

Eugene Bear Heart

Bison Attack Indian Horses
Adapted from a painting by George Catlin (1796-1872)

the buffalo, and it fell to its knees. We were all yelling, and the dust was so thick I could hardly see. I tried for one more buffalo but could not get it down. The other Indians were all shooting buffalo. We killed over a hundred buffalo that day. That was enough, so we did not kill any more. The women came and helped skin the buffalo. It took about an hour to skin and dress one. They used knives that had been bought from white traders.

We wrapped the meat up in the hides and carried it back to camp on travois or on horseback, as we did not have wagons. The hides were tanned; some of the meat eaten raw, some cooked, and some cut in strips and dried. Some of the dried meat was pounded between rocks, mixed with wild berries. Big chunks of this were placed in a basket made of buffalo skin and stored. This meat would keep for over a year. When the meat was brought into camp, everyone could take what they wanted.

Most of our horses were taken from the Crow Indians, with whom we were continually fighting back and forth. I was nineteen years of age when I went on my first horse raid. During the next six years I took part in three horse raids and two Indian fights.

Our camp was in Montana at that time. On my first horse raid nine other young men went with me. We dressed up in war clothes and put

Horse Raiding and Buffalo Hunting

on war paint. We rode for about five days southwest toward the Crow land. We kept a careful guard all the time so we would not be seen.

On the sixth day we located a Crow village. We then hid our horses in some trees and started out on foot, over the hills. The grass was high, and we were able to crawl and walk along without being seen. The Crow horses were grazing about on the hills around the camp. We managed to catch eleven of these Crow horses and slowly lead them away.

We were tricky, so we got away without being seen. That was the only time we went on foot. The other horse raids were made at night and were not so dangerous. I went out on some of these raids. Thirty or more would go on these raids. Three or four days riding would take us into Crow territory, and we had to be very careful, as the Crows were looking for us. Any Crow Indians we found were surrounded and killed. We would not attack a Crow village but would find out where they herded their horses and in the night or early morning would go in and drive the horses away. If there were any guards, we would kill them if we could. We then started for our own camp as fast as we could. Sometimes we had to let the horses go and were lucky to escape. The Crows also raided us Sioux, and sometimes small hunting parties of Sioux were all killed by the Crows.

The fights I was in took place when I was out with a band on the warpath looking for trouble. In one fight we surprised a band of Crows, and in a running fight we killed all the Crows except one. He was too fast and escaped. We scalped the eleven dead Crows and got most of their horses. My horse was wounded in this fight but got all right later. Three Sioux were killed in this fight and three wounded. All the fighting took place on horseback. The Crows did not stop to make a stand, and they were shot down when they tried to escape. Three Crows were killed at once when two of them stopped to help another who was wounded and falling from his horse.

Some of the Sioux stopped to kill these three, and the rest of us kept right on after the other Crows. We chased the one Crow who escaped for many miles but finally had to give up.

Frank Bull Bear

When Worlds Collide

Frank Bull Bear

My grandparents did not want me to go to school or learn the ways of the white people.

Frank Bull Bear, a Lakota, was born in eastern Montana in 1869 while his band, consisting of thirty-five lodges, was on a buffalo hunt. His father was injured on that hunt and died in 1870. Bull Bear's grandparents reared him. As a child and young man, he bitterly resented the influence of white culture on Indian ways. In 1895 he married Annie Two Shields and farmed and raised cattle and horses into the mid-1910s.

MY GRANDPARENTS WERE GOOD TO ME. I did not have to do any work. I spent all my time playing games of war, hunting, and riding. Our war games were rough. We used sticks and bows with blunt arrows. We also used rocks when we became angry. Once in a while one of us would get hurt. Then there would be a commotion in camp. The mother of the boy who was hurt would shriek at the top of her voice and try to catch or hit us. My grandparents always took my part so I ran to them when I got into trouble.

The other boys and I hunted rabbits and birds near the camp. We used small bows and sharp arrows. We sneaked up to within ten or twenty yards of the game before we shot.

My grandfather's tipi was made of hides. It was round and about ten feet in diameter. Buffalo and deer hides were placed on the ground. Our clothes were made of skins. Extra clothing was tied in a bundle.

During the summer we moved from place to place. When I was about six years old, my grandfather gave me a small pony which I rode bareback. When we traveled, we went single file. The hunters led the way. Our tents were loaded on a travois and pulled by a horse. Some of the women walked along leading the horse. There were about a hundred or more dogs. The dogs stayed close to the end of the line when we were on the march. Dogs that would not behave while we were marching were beaten or killed. If it was a pet, the owner tied its mouth with buckskin so it could not bark. Sometimes camp was made after we had marched only half a day, and sometimes we marched all day. Camp was usually made by a stream. It did not take long to put up the tipis. The women did the work. The men looked after the horses. I and some of the other children would go down and play in the stream.

We always had plenty to eat. My grandfather was too old to hunt, but the hunters gave us chunks of meat. Some of it we ate raw or roasted over a fire. Thin strips were hung in the sun to dry.

When winter set in, we moved into the woods near a river. We had dried meat, dried plums, choke cherries, and bull berries to eat. An open fire was built on the ground in the center of the tipi. This kept us warm, but when the fire went out at night, the tent was very cold. Buffalo robes kept us warm. Some mornings I woke up with my head covered with snow that had fallen through the opening at the top of the tipi.

At this time the Indians were strong and healthy. They did not know what sickness was. In the winter time we wore moccasins, breech cloth, mittens, and a cap that covered our ears and neck. Parts of our bodies were exposed to the weather, but we did not get sick.

When I was eight years old, we traveled to Fort Yates, Dakota Territory. I think the trip took us about twenty-five days or more. Our hunters shot deer, buffalo, and antelope on the way. Most of them used bow and arrow, but we had two or three guns in the camp. I rode my pony the entire way. I did not know at the time where we were going. On nearing Fort Yates we pitched camp about two miles from the fort. Up

Frank Bull Bear

to this time I had never seen a white man. Two or three days later I went with my grandfather to the fort. I saw white soldiers and was afraid. My grandfather told me not to be afraid as these people were our friends. We were given rations consisting of flour, bacon, coffee, and sugar.

The first flour we received was thrown away but we kept the sack. The bacon we tried to roast over a fire. It was too salty, and we fed it to our dogs. I ate most of the sugar but did not like the coffee at the time. A few days after this my grandfather and I went in for beef rations.

When we reached Fort Yates, there were four or five hundred Indians waiting. The cattle were grazing down by the Missouri River. One beef was divided among four families. We were given orders to wait until the cattle were shot by Indian police and soldiers before we went over the bank. About one hundred head was killed. When the first cow was shot, the Indians started over the bank and could not be stopped. The Indians all knew the other families with whom they were to share the beef. There was much confusion before everyone finally was busy with the butchering. I did not like the smell of the cattle and neither did I like the meat. My grandfather took his share of the meat home. We still had some dried buffalo and deer meat to eat. We ate this and dried most of the beef. After the beef was dried, it did not taste so bad. We got beef rations about every two weeks.

We lived near Fort Yates for four years. During that time we became used to the rations issued at the fort. I did not go to school at all. I did not want to go and my grandparents did not want me to go either.

From Fort Yates we moved up near the Cannon Ball Substation. My grandfather built a log house which we used in the wintertime.

My days of play were over now as I had to go to school. An Indian policeman came to our cabin and took me in a wagon to the school. There were about twenty-five children in the school. I did not like it at all. The next day I started off to school but went down to the woods along the Missouri River where I played all day. The next morning I started for the woods again but was caught by the policeman just as I got to the woods. I cried, but he made me go with him to the school. Every day the first month the policeman brought in five or six children. The first year in school I learned only a few words of English. Some of us brought bows and arrows to school but our teacher, Mr. A. C. Wells, took them away from us. He was afraid we would get hurt with them.

At this time my hair grew down to my shoulders. One day Mr. Wells cut my hair very short. I did not like it at all. He cut the hair of every boy who had long hair. I went to this school for five years. I did not learn much of anything. I liked to hunt and ride on horseback. After school was out I forgot all about it. My grandparents did not want me to go to school or learn the ways of the white people.

After I quit school, I spent my time hunting and riding. I hunted deer along the Missouri River. Every year I shot five to fifteen deer. I used a muzzle-loading gun that shot one ball. It was fairly accurate up to fifty yards. I killed most of the deer in the wintertime when there was snow on the ground so I could track them. I hunted antelope and rabbits north of the Cannonball River. Sometimes about one hundred of us went on an antelope or rabbit hunt.

Before the hunt took place, we held a powwow. We decided who was to be the leader, where we were to hunt, and how long we wanted to stay. We then chose a person to go to the agent and inform him of our intentions as it was necessary to get permission to leave the reservation. The agent then decided who could go on the hunt. If any of the Indians had been in trouble such as drinking, fighting or were unruly, they were not allowed to leave the reservation. One or two policemen went with us on the hunt, mainly to see that we came back to the reservation on time. We knew better than to molest or steal from the white people.

The best hunt I was on took place a year or two before Sitting Bull was killed. Old Man Elk was chosen leader. About one hundred and fifty hunters, women, and children, went on the hunt. My grandparents did not go so I went with my friends, the Black Hoops. Elk gave orders that we would leave about six in the morning. We were to meet at the crossing on the Cannonball River at the Parkin Ranch. Early that morning the Indians came on horseback, wagons, and travois. The Indian policeman, Follows the Road, gave the order to start. Elk led the way on his horse. We fell in line single file behind him. We passed through the Parkin Ranch, and Elk led the way northwest across the hills. Five miles after passing the ranch we saw small bands of antelope, but we did not make any attempt to kill any.

Frank Bull Bear

A Little fresh meat for the Indians: taken before the opening of the Rosebud Reservation, near Winner, South Dakota, 1880.
Adapted from a photograph in the Fred Hultstrand History in Pictures Collection, NDIRS-NDSU, Fargo.

    We marched all day long, only stopping to water our horses at a creek. We made camp on a creek near the present site of St. Anthony. The women put up the tents, and the children gathered wood for the camp fires.

    The hunt started the next morning. There were about seventy-five hunters. Elk told each hunter which way and how far to go. Most of the hunters had bows and arrows, while about ten of us had guns. Each hunter also had a club fastened to his horse. We spread out in a circle of about five miles. We then rode toward the center, and we yelled and made as much noise as we could. Bands of antelope, rabbits, and an occasional coyote dashed ahead of us. They were all very wild, and we did not kill many on the drive. As we closed in and the circle became smaller, the antelope became more frightened than ever. The antelope tried to dash through our lines. A few got away, but most of them were killed or wounded. Two coyotes were killed as they tried to break through. The rabbits milled around as we drew closer. When we got within fifty yards of them, we closed in on foot and used our clubs. They ran in all directions, but we killed most of them. That day we killed about sixty antelope, two hundred rabbits, and two coyotes. After the hunt the women arrived with the wagons. The antelope and rabbits

When Worlds Collide

were butchered on the spot. The meat was divided up, each family getting one antelope and three rabbits. That night we had a big feast. Some of the meat was roasted on sticks over the fires. We ate as much as we could. That night we held a dance that lasted almost until morning. The next day the women cut up the meat and hung it on poles to dry in the sun. A few hunters went out and killed more antelope. The rest stayed in camp and practiced shooting with bow and arrow. We put up rabbit skins on sticks and shot at them from a distance of fifty to one hundred yards. I was not a very good shot with the bow.

We had one more big hunt before going back to the reservation and killed about fifty antelope and two or three hundred rabbits. Everyone was happy, and we did not have any fights. On the fifth day out Elk led us back to the reservation. Here we had a big feast for the others that had not taken part in the hunt.

The Indians around the Cannon Ball Agency were friendly to the white people. We took no part in the Sitting Bull trouble. We knew he was a trouble maker, and we had nothing to do with him or his Indians.

In 1895 I married Annie Two Shields. We moved eight miles south of the Cannon Ball Subagency where I tried farming and raised cattle and horses. I broke about five acres of sod and planted corn, potatoes, squash, and pumpkins. By 1900 I had twenty head of cattle and fifteen head of horses. I put up a few tons of hay in the summer. I did not need much as my stock grazed in the woods along the Missouri River. I made a good living until 1915. At that time many white settlers came in. Many of my Indian friends quit raising cattle and horses. They leased or sold their land to white people. They no longer did any work. As was the custom when hungry, they came to my house and I killed a beef for them. Gradually my cattle disappeared, and by 1920 I did not have a cow. I sold all my horses except one team. In 1925 I moved up near the Cannon Ball Substation as I no longer was making anything on my land.

Robert Charbonneau

Life Around Fort Totten

Robert Charbonneau

The Indians died like flies.

Robert Charbonneau was born in 1861 at St. Joseph, the oldest son of Baptiste Charbonneau and Victoria Vondel. Victoria Vondel was born at Fort Garry, Canada, in 1814 into the family of a French fur trader and Chippewa mother. Robert's father was Baptiste who died at Fort Totten in 1868. According to Robert, shortly before his mother, Victoria, died at age 104 in 1918, she told him, a half-sister, and Father Ambrose, the priest at St. Michael's mission, that Baptiste, on his deathbed in 1868, had revealed that he was the son of Touissant Charbonneau and Sacagawea, "the bird woman," who made the journey with Lewis and Clark. Baptiste had sworn Victoria to secrecy. This revelation created quite a stir in the WPA interview office, and every effort was made to authenticate Robert Charbonneau's story, with little success since many church records had been lost or burned over the years. Father Ambrose in 1927 confirmed Victoria's deathbed revelation. "She was very feeble at the time she brought up the subject," he testified. "However, I always found her very truthful in all that she told me of the past." Recent scholarship, however, does not support the claim that Robert's father was **the** Baptiste Charbonneau who was Sacagawea's son. Newspaper reports present evidence that Sacagawea's Baptiste died in 1866 on his way from Oregon to the Montana gold fields.

REMEMBER THE TRIP [St. Joseph to Fort Totten] quite well. We traveled much the same as any of the Indians, using two-wheel carts and Indian ponies. We had two of these carts of

13

Life Around Fort Totten

Fort Totten on Devils Lake
Sketch shows layout of the fort as it appeared shortly after construction in 1867 (SHSND 78.121).

our own. There were two other families that came at the same time, Ashurs and Belgardes.

They took their time on this trip, taking nearly two weeks before reaching the Fort [Totten]. Father and the other men hunted along the way.

At that time there were still buffalo to be seen roaming around. I don't remember seeing any on that trip, but the men killed geese, ducks, chickens, and crane, more than they could eat; but the women cleaned and dried them for future use. They split the ducks and chickens in two, the geese in smaller pieces stringing them on a line fastened from the tent to a cart. They would take the line down when they were on the move, putting it up at the next stop.

When we got to our destination, the old log fort was still in use, but soon after this they started building the present fort.

Father squatted on land about a half mile northeast of the fort in the woods near the lake shore. He built a log house, chinking it with clay. The house, when completed, was approximately twenty-five by fifty feet, with a fireplace in the north end.

This took between two and three months. After this was completed and the family moved in, father went to work at the fort, helping wherever he was needed. He worked here until fall when he was taken ill, dying some time in the latter part of November or early December 1868. Before he passed away, General Whistler came to see him, giving him papers on the land. These papers were to give the family possession of the land when it was surveyed, but up to the present time there has never been a survey and now after sixty-nine years the authorities are trying to put me and my family off from this land.

When I was sixteen, I went to work for Frank Palmer, owner of the store at Fort Totten; and that same year, my mother, Victoria, married a man by the name of Belland, a French trapper and guide. There were two girls born to this union, Louise and Mary.

I worked for Palmer for thirty years, drove the mail stage from the fort to Lake Belleau, fifty miles southwest of Fort Totten where I met the mail from Jamestown.

Driving stage in the summer was easy, but when winter came and the mail had to go, regardless of the weather, it was not so easy. I always changed teams, or rather, horses (I drove four horses, one team latched to the stage, the other team in front of the pole team) at the Eli Prescott Farm, where Palmer kept relay horses.

In the summer and nice weather, I could make the trip to Lake Belleau and return, a distance of approximately one hundred miles, in from six to eight days, depending on how things went on the trip.

I always stayed one night at Eli Prescott's, going and coming, the other nights camping wherever night overtook me. We very seldom carried passengers as the stage was a mail stage and Frank Palmer's freight stage, bringing all store supplies. There were other stage drivers working for Palmer. I would leave early one morning; in two days another stage would leave, and two days later another, bringing mail to the fort about every three days.

During the winter months, when it was not possible for horses to get through, Lomass, who also worked for Palmer, made the entire trip all the way to Jamestown with dog teams and sleds, bringing the mail but no freight. The freight for winter was all hauled in before winter set in. I was substitute for Lomass if he was not able to go.

I did not have to go very often, perhaps twice or three times during the winter, and I do not remember ever being caught in a real blizzard on any of these trips, but that it was plenty hard at any time, temperature often at 40° below. I wore fur garments and shoe packs, fur-lined, with heavy wool socks under them that mother knit for me from wool that she carded and spun herself. Palmer bought the shoe packs for the men from the Indians who made them. The nights on these trips, I slept out, in a fur-lined sleeping bag.

I would find a place in the lee side of a hill or in some hollow, dig a place in the snow, build a fire if there was any wood I could gather up, and always tried to find a place where wood could be gotten. After getting something to eat for myself and feeding the dogs, I would crawl into my sleeping bag and get what rest I could.

This entire trip, approximately two hundred miles, usually took three weeks if every thing went right. In 1883, I was held up for three days by a blizzard but was lucky enough to be at the Prescott Farm at the time.

As a boy one of my earliest recollections is of seeing the buffalo going to the lake [Devils Lake] shore to drink, only a short distance from our house, possibly less than a quarter-mile. One spring sometime in the 1870s the Indians came into the hills surrounding the fort and camped, while the men hunted. Among these were Chief Coming Cloud. One morning the buffalo came to the lake shore, and Coming Cloud killed one of them. The Indians skinned and quartered the buffalo, took it to their camping place, and proceeded to have a feast. They had not been eating much meat during the winter months, nor too much of anything, as it was an especially hard winter, and Coming Cloud ate so much that he became violently ill, and that night he died. The wailing was something terrible after this happened.

The Indians' idea of mourning the dead was to make a terrible wailing noise, the women doing the wailing. Coming Cloud's widow went off on a hillside by herself to wail and slash her arms and legs with a knife.

This the soldiers put a stop to as they did not want the Indians to become excited, fearing an outbreak; the Indians were more or less restless still.

Robert Charbonneau

In a day or two the Indians left, taking the body of Coming Cloud back to the reservation for burial, where they could mourn and perform their burial rites without interference from the white man.

I sat and conversed with Sitting Bull, who came to the Fort Totten reservation several different times.

I do not know why Sitting Bull came to the fort; the officers feared to have him mingling with Indians on the reservation as he never failed to stir up trouble, the Indians being very restless after one of his visits. My memory of Sitting Bull is a homely, stupid, Sioux Indian but I guess that Sitting Bull was smarter than he looked.

When I was a boy, I used to be around the soldiers' quarters whenever I got the chance, and the bugler taught me to blow the different calls on the bugle, and a great many times I would blow the calls for the bugler. At times some of the soldiers would come for me to perform this duty when the bugler would be too drunk to do it himself. This is the nearest to belonging to the army that I ever came.

In cold, stormy weather the soldiers had a rope from the quarters to the wood pile and each man would be detailed to go after a stick of wood and they would keep this up until the officer in command thought there was fuel enough to last the night out. It was 40° below for two months at a time, and storms every time the wind blew, which was most of the time.

The suffering among the Indians at this time of the year was bad. One year there was a smallpox epidemic on the reservation. I think it was 1883. I was working at Frank Palmer's at this time, having gone to work for Palmer in 1877. The people at the post, and there were many Indian families in the woods near the fort, were not allowed to leave the post for any purpose.

The Indians who had this disease knew it was what they called "black death," and when a member of a family contracted the disease, they would leave home and go to a draw near Fort Totten, one and a half miles northeast of the fort.

Father Jerome worked night and day on the reservation vaccinating, caring for the ones who were down, carrying food to the homes that were afflicted, in fact doing everything for them, spiritually and physically; but in spite of all that could be done, the Indians died like flies. In

Life Around Fort Totten

this coulee, years afterwards, there were still skeletons of Indians to be found. It was during this epidemic that the Indians held what was the last Sun Dance, and the soldiers allowed it because of the unrest on the reservation.

Father Jerome worked the hardest of any man I ever knew. I met Father Jerome a great many times, when I was carrying mail, many miles from the mission, either with a team of ponies and buggy or if the weather was too stormy, on horseback.

Father Jerome never seemed to tire, going early and late, when he was called to Devils Lake and even to Rolla in times of extreme illness and when the parish priest would be away on some other case. He would often come into the store before leaving for the reservation or some other point where they had sent for him.

When we Charbonneaus came to Fort Totten, we built quite near the lake shore, approximately a quarter-mile from the shore; now the lake shore is over a mile away.

The house that father built in 1868 burned in 1880. At this time the log building used as a bakery for the soldiers was abandoned. It was only a few rods from our home; and after the fire, we moved into this building. It is a log house approximately twenty-five by thirty feet. The logs are snow white and it is chinked with yellow clay. I built a lean-to on the west side, but to get into the original house you have to go up a step. This step is a stone slab, the one put there when the house was built.

In 1884 or 1885 the soldiers and people at the fort decided to put on a Fourth of July celebration. The soldiers fixed up the parade grounds adjoining the square on the west. They planned a ball game, the soldiers against the civilians. The Indians were to put on a show battle. At sunrise the fort fired a salute and kept up the gunfire for about half an hour. About nine o'clock the settlers in the surrounding country were beginning to come in.

Most of these people came in wagons, some driving oxen, others horses. The whole family packed in the wagon along with feed for the horses and a huge lunch. They parked in the rear of Palmer Store, a large open place sloping west to the trail that led to Lake Belleau. The government boat made a trip across the lake to Devils Lake bringing back a load of people who came from north and east of the lake.

Robert Charbonneau

Soon the Indians started coming to the fort. The men on their ponies, the ponies all decked out in bright blankets and fancy bridles, and the men in their beaded clothes, head feathers, and war paint. The women and children came in carts or walking, all in their brightest colored clothing.

At eleven o'clock there was a parade; first the soldiers in companies, and after them came the Indians on their ponies. The fort band led the parade. After this some of the officers talked to the crowd on the progress the territory was making and the hope of soon becoming a state and on the friendly relations between the white man and his red brothers. The band played "America," everyone singing. After this came the ball game, the soldiers winning. Then every one left to eat their lunch.

At two o'clock the show battle started between the two groups of Indians. They looked very warlike. The battle was fought with guns loaded only with blank cartridges. When the battle had been going on for about thirty minutes, the spectators noticed a commotion on the field but were unable to make out what the trouble was about.

I managed to worm my way pretty close to where the trouble was and found that one Indian had carried a loaded gun and, getting behind his enemy, had shot him. I did not linger there very long for the Indians, whom I could understand, were all for going on the warpath, killing the friends of the Indian who did the shooting, taking over the fort, and incidentally scalping a few of their white brothers. I made my way to Major McLaughlin to tell him what I had heard, but by the time I found him the soldiers had trained the cannons on the Indians. The soldiers were in the field disarming the Indians and ordering them back to the reservation. They arrested the Indian, Iron Horse, who did the killing, putting him under armed guard in the guard house to keep him from being killed. The civilians were ordered to go home, most of them only too anxious to get to their homes to protect their property. The mourning Indians wailing, the men threatening and all out unmanageable, and the women howling and wailing. Finally, the next day, they got the Indians back on the reservation, and things quieted.

Hunting, Trapping, Guiding, and the Circus, Too

Hunting, Trapping, Guiding, and the Circus, Too

Michael Davis

To us hunting was our work and an important one, yes <u>the</u> necessary one.

> Michael Davis was one of eight children born (1852) to William Davis, a Chippewa, and Marie Enneau, who was French-Chippewa (referred to at the time as half-blood or later as Métis). Because William Davis guided wagon trains to the Montana gold fields and got his family involved in circus work, young Michael's childhood was not typical; his life beyond his early years, however, reflects the traditional Chippewa ways. He was a lifelong hunter, and his description of the buffalo hunt and life on it is exceptional. He reflects the adjustment from a free life on the prairie and plains to living on a small reservation.

WHILE A BOY AT ST. JOE, I used to go out on the buffalo hunt. As many as three hundred carts would go out on the hunts. My father had five horses and five oxen with a corresponding number of carts. When we were on the march, we went three carts abreast. We hunted all over the prairie between Devils Lake and the Mouse River. We generally made three hunts each season. In the first part of June we started out the first time and stayed out during June and July. On this hunt we were especially after the bulls until July 20. After that we left the bulls alone and killed only cows. Then we went back with the meat. In August and September we were again out hunting. Of the meat we obtained this time, we made pemmican and dry meat. I was along three or four times to Winnipeg but never went to St. Paul. Going to St. Paul was a dangerous undertaking as the Sioux were watching the trail all summer, waylaying as many as they possibly could. In October we started out on the third hunt. The object this time was to lay in a supply of fresh meat. For this reason we remained out until the weather was very cold, in fact so cold that the meat would keep without being made into pemmican. The pemmican and dry meat was sold for about five or six cents a pound. During the fall hunt we would also trap foxes, wolves, prairie dogs, minks, otters, and beavers and take any other game we could get. These hunts were not always successful in finding buffalo. With so many people in one group and no place to obtain supplies, the food would soon run out. When this happened, we would have to dig prairie turnips and eat them. It can easily be imagined what a tremendous task it was to find and dig those turnips for hundreds of people. There were lots of pot holes, sloughs, and lakes in which waterfowl nested. The eggs found in the nests were a welcome addition to the menu. The birds themselves also formed a part of the diet.

Buffalo hunting was well-organized. It had to be. We had good rules. If a man killed too many buffalo, he was fined five dollars. If he allowed any meat to spoil, he was fined the same amount. The hunt had a chief, a council, and a captain. The latter had three men always at his command. When we were on the march, six men acted as scouts. Two rode out from the column to the left, two to the right, and two ahead. It was their duty to watch out for hostile Indians and locate water for a suitable campsite. In the evening the council met to decide who was to act as scouts the following day. After a permanent camp had been made, scouts were sent out to locate buffalo. If we happened to get near a herd when we were on the march, we immediately went into camp and prepared for the hunt. When the scouts located buffalo after camp had been pitched, they would either ride back to camp and report or they would ride back and forth on a ridge so that they could be seen from the camp. In case they located hostile Indians instead of buffalo, they rode back and forth and took off their coats or jackets and waved them up and down. We always attempted to locate the camp near a lake, a stream, or a spring. In small lakes the water was not always fit to use because of the large number of buffalo that were wading through it and drinking out of it. We also had to find grass. Sometimes we had to go quite a distance because the buffalo had eaten all of the grass. Thus we had many things that had to be taken into consideration. When we think about hunting today, we think of it as a sport. There was no sport to it to us. To us hunting was work, and an important one, yes, *the* necessary one. Then there was fuel. If camp could not be located near timber, we used buffalo chips. Horses were specially trained for hunting buffalo. When these horses saw a herd of buffalo, the riders had all they could do to hold them back until the time came to charge the herd. It was dangerous to ride right in among the animals. I have seen riders and horses go down under the hooves of the maddened beasts.

When the hunt was over for the day, the carts went out from the camp to get the meat. The men skinned the animals, and the women and children loaded the meat on the carts. After it had been brought to the camp, the meat was cut up into thin slices and hung out on racks to dry. When it was dry enough, it was either packed away as dry meat or else pounded on a buffalo hide turned green-side-up until it was made into small crumbs, after which it was mixed with buffalo grease and then packed into sacks made of buffalo hides. This was pemmican. Knives used by the Indians in their hunting were of two kinds, one small-handled for skinning, and another large "ax" knife strong enough to cut bones and small pieces of wood. For the latter, however, they used small hatchets more. The large knives were about eighteen inches long, including the handle. They cost five dollars each. The hunts I described above were made on the Dakota prairies. In Montana it was hard to get up close to the buffalo. They stayed in valleys and arroyos. From these they had to be led or driven out on the flat or level places where the horsemen could get up to them. It was almost impossible to drive them out, but they could easily be led. All a man had to do was to ride as close to them as possible, let out a yell, and start away from them, and they would follow. I became quite adept at this.

If our hunting party was caught far from home in the late fall and could not get back, we made log shacks with fireplaces of mud and stones. In these improvised ovens, we roasted meat in large chunks and prepared our other food as well. The ovens also warmed our shacks.

When I was still a small boy at St. Joe, my father fought the Sioux several times. Once he killed four Sioux on Sioux Coulee between Langdon and Cavalier. He brought home a buffalo robe that he took from one of the warriors he killed.

I was eleven years old when our family went to Fort Wadsworth, Dakota Territory. Although I was young, I got two dollars a day for helping to put up hay. The Sioux were always hanging around, and it was hard to get anyone to risk going out to work in the open. My father always kept the gun handy. In 1865, when I was thirteen, I accompanied a cart train made up of miners from Fort Abercrombie, Dakota Territory, to Helena, Montana. The carts were drawn by horses. My father and a man named Parisien were hired as guides to lead the train over the right route. For this they got ten dollars a day. Colonel Holmes, Major Peck, and Captain Dick were the leaders of the train which was composed mostly of white men.

Our party of miners was fired on by the Sioux, the Blackfeet, and the prairie Big Bellies or Gros Ventre (Hidatsa), but no one was killed or even hurt until we reached the Missouri River. At that point there was a large Sioux camp. One of the white men, an Englishman, went to the Sioux and bought some stuff from them. On the way back to our group, a Sioux fired at him and hit his arm. Our family and the Parisien family camped outside the corral, as we had to take care of the horses. The oxen and cows were placed inside the ring of carts. Father had three oxen and two cows, and Parisien had one ox. There were only three horses, and they were saddle horses. When we were out on the open prairie, we did not post guards, but if we were close to timber, we did, on four sides of the camp, two men in each place. I was going out after dark to see about the horses, and on going out of the tipi I felt something on the ground. I found it to be a man. I immediately called father who in turn called the leaders of the miners. They talked to the man in several Indian languages, but he did not answer. They could not get a word out of him. By signs they made him understand that if they ran across him again, they would shoot him. The white men said they had no right to kill him at that time, since he had not resisted when he was caught. When our party resumed the journey in the morning, he sat where we left him as long as we could see him.

It took our party three months to go from the James River to Helena. After the wagon train had safely reached the Rockies at Helena, we went south about a hundred miles and spent the winter. All winter the men hunted deer, mountain sheep, elk, and bears. The next year we returned to Dakota Territory between Fort Berthold and Fort Union to hunt buffalo. When we returned in 1866, we went to Fort Totten which was about ready when we reached that place in the fall.

While the Sioux were hostile to the white people, the Cree, the Chippewa, and the mixed-bloods were friendly to them. Our family located about four miles from Fort Totten. One evening a number of freighters on their way from Fort Totten to Fort Abercrombie stopped at our home. The freighters had forgotten to buy baking soda at Fort Totten. They gave me three dollars to go back to the fort and get some for them during the night. On account of the Sioux hanging around all the time, this was a dangerous thing to do, but I got through all right. In 1867 we went to the Yellow Medicine River in Minnesota to look for buffalo and spent the following winter there. In the summer of 1868 we hired out to a circus owned by one Captain Waldron and went with him to Iowa where the circus left us stranded without paying us a cent of the nine hundred dollars we had coming. We went along as Indian dancers. The following winter we stayed on Spirit Lake in Iowa. In 1869 we returned to Yellow Medicine River in Minnesota and stayed there for four years. From there we went to the White Earth Reservation in Minnesota where we spent three years.

In 1876, the year Custer was killed, we came back to Fort Totten. In 1877 we heard of buffalo near present-day Minot. Ten families with forty carts started west and went as far as Montana where we remained for seven years. On our way into Montana, we crossed the Milk River and hunted buffalo with the Gros Ventre and the Assiniboines at Bear Paw near Fort Belknap. I shot most of my buffalo between the Missouri and the Yellowstone rivers. There was a large number of them there. I bought a wild horse from a man who came down from the Rocky Mountains and trained it for running buffalo. It took some time before I could control it as I should. On two occasions while the horse was yet only party trained, I was caught in a tight place while hunting the animals. At one time the horse ran right in among the buffalo and was surrounded by the herd. The captain of the hunt shouted to the other hunters: "Don't shoot!" But the noise was so great and the dust so thick that they could neither hear the warning nor see the danger I was in. Several shots were fired so that the bullets whined close by me. Finally I got out of it. I was so scared that I shot only one buffalo. Another time I got in between the herd and the steep bank of a ravine and was almost pushed over the precipice by the animals. I was scared this time also, so that I could shoot only one buffalo. I was thrown from my horse twice while hunting buffalo. Once I was riding at full speed when I came to a steep bank of a ravine. The horse made as if to jump across it, but changed his mind at the last minute and stopped so suddenly that I flew over its head across the draw.

Not far from Fort Assiniboine, Sitting Bull camped with a large band of Sioux in 1878, two years after Custer was killed. I saw him there. The captain at the fort went out to him and asked if he would not settle down on a reservation and give up fights with the white men. The captain offered him and his people horses, cattle, and everything that would be needed. But Sitting Bull replied that he did not want help. All he wanted was to have the buffalo on the prairies and that the white men leave him and his people alone. He said: "When I was home in the Black Hills, I did not quit until my arm got tired of hitting the white men."

While in Montana I saw Riel, the leader of the Indian rebellion in Canada, several times. At Carrol, Montana, Riel called me over to him one day and asked me if I could get a young girl to take a few drops of whiskey. He said, "I have tried to get her to drink a little of it, but she won't do it." The girl was a daughter of my cousin. I said I could get her to do it. After coaxing her a little while, the girl took a few drops of the liquor. A couple of days later Riel and the girl were married. I thought that Riel must have put a love potion in the whiskey.

After our stay in Montana, we came back to the Turtle Mountains in Dakota Territory in 1884 where I trapped for about ten years — muskrats, minks, skunks, foxes, and coyotes. I have shot at least a thousand buffalo. At one time in Montana I had two hundred buffalo hides in my possession. I had shot practically all the animals from which these hides had been taken. Fourteen was the largest number of buffalo I shot in one day.

I knew Chief Red Thunder. In 1862 a treaty was to be made at Grand Forks. A large number of Chippewa and mixed-bloods, among them our family and Red Thunder, went there to be present at the making of the treaty. While we were there a cart train of freighters came through. Red Thunder and his Indians stopped them and took everything away from them. He had the oxen killed and the meat, together with the supplies carried in the train, distributed among his people.

When the trouble occurred at the Michael Lagan shack near St. John in 1895, and Red Thunder was arrested, I was in a party of between fifty and a hundred who started out from Belcourt to go to the assistance of the chief. East of Belcourt we were met by the Indian agent who told us that everything had been settled and that all was over, so we turned back.

The trouble started with the county trying to collect taxes from the Indians and mixed-bloods. The Indians had cattle and horses that they had gotten from the government. Some of these the sheriff took for taxes. The sheriff, Tom Flynn, had taken a government ox from Charley Gladue for taxes. Neither the ox nor the money for it was returned to Gladue. Antoine Enneau had two mules and a cow. The sheriff took the cow for taxes. The sheriff told the people that if they did not pay the taxes, they had to get off the land. The white people used the tax situation as a club over the Indians to make them get off the land and crowd together in the two townships set aside as a reservation.

Eagle Staff

Trouble with the Crow

Eagle Staff

. . . we killed all of them except one man.

>Eagle Staff was born near present-day Stanton in 1865. His father, Coming Horse, who was born near Pipestone, was that time in a battle with the Crows. Because he killed a Crow chief who carried an eagle staff, he named his son Eagle Staff. Eagle Staff's brief memoir illustrates the importance of the hunt and the animosity between the Crow and Lakota people.

MY BOYHOOD WAS ABOUT THE SAME AS OTHER INDIAN BOYS, playing games and taking care of horses. There were about one thousand people in our camp. Many families would leave camp and go on hunting trips. Some were going and coming all the time on hunting trips. The hills at this time were covered with all kinds of wild game.

When I was nine years old, I was taken on many hunting trips. One time the camp was attacked by the Crows. I was very badly frightened. Many were killed, and the Crows were finally driven away. The Crows did most of the attacking.

The fastest horses were used on the hunts because the buffalo would outrun an ordinary horse. We had a few guns, but most of our hunters used bows and arrows. A good man might kill a buffalo with one arrow, but it usually took two or three. Once in a while a wounded buffalo would attack the horse and rider and kill them. I went on my

Trouble with the Crow

Crow Warriors

first buffalo hunt with my father when I was thirteen years old. I tried to kill a buffalo calf but did not succeed. Father brought down two buffalo with bow and arrows that day. Two buffalo herds numbered from a few to over two hundred buffalo.

When I was thirteen, our entire camped moved westward. In one fight with the Crows, we killed all of them except one man. This man got away and swam across a river. We could have killed him, but he was so brave that we let him go.

French traders came down from the north, and I traded my horse for a good rifle. I did not have any trouble killing lots of game after I did.

The only time my life was in danger was on a buffalo hunt. My horse stepped in a hole and fell, throwing me off. Buffalo ran all around me, and as I had hurt my back, I could not move. The others tied me on a horse and took me back to camp.

In about 1880, I and other Indians came back and settled near what is now Cannon Ball. I have lived here ever since. I am a very good at making drums, rattles, etc. No one in particular taught me how to do this, but I learned by watching others.

A Lakota Childhood

Follows the Road

The boys did about as they pleased, but the girls had to do some work.

Follows the Road was born about 1870 in the Killdeer Mountains where her people had established a permanent camp. When she was thirteen years old, the Lakota in the Killdeer Mountains were moved to the Standing Rock Reservation where her family lived near Fort Yates. She remembers a childhood of some work and some play.

AS A GIRL I PLAYED GAMES WITH THE OTHER CHILDREN. Different games were made of willows. Tops were made from the ends of buffalo horns and a rawhide string was used to spin it. The boys did about as they pleased, but the girls had to do some work. I had to peel bark from willow sticks, dig wild vegetables, carry water, and help mother in many ways.

I had two pets: one was a bear cub, given to me by my father. It was a nice pet, but as it got older it became rough and had to be shot. I gave it to grandfather [that it, returned the bear to his creator]. The other pet was a skunk. I tied a string around its neck, and we would go out in the hills. The skunk would catch grasshoppers and worms, and I thought that it was lots of fun.

When I was a little girl, I was very much afraid of the Crows, Arikara, and Blackfeet as they were enemies. Many times these Indians would sneak up on our camp in the night, enter some of the tipis and kill the occupants, scalp them, steal horses, and be gone before the rest of

A Lakota Childhood

the camp knew anything about it. Sometimes the camp had out guards, and the enemy Indians were surprised. In the fight that followed most of the enemy would be killed and scalped.

Father went on many horse raids, sometimes as far as seven or eight hundred miles away. He managed to get about thirty horses in this manner. He killed many enemy Indians but did not take part in any of the battles with the white people.

One of my brothers died of the nose bleed. The medicine man came to help him and went through many ceremonies, but could not help him any, and he bled to death.

When I was about thirteen years of age the camp moved from the Killdeer Mountains to Fort Yates. We lived in the woods, and the Indians were issued rations and many things to help us get along without hunting. We did not like this kind of food at first and could hardly eat the beef.

My father did a little work around the fort and was given a bugle by one of the soldiers. When father died, he was buried on a scaffold placed on four poles. His body was wrapped in buffalo hides and deerskins. An American flag was placed over him, and his bugle was placed on one of the posts.

My mother lived to be over one hundred years old. She died twice, once when I was a child. We left her for dead in the tipi, and the camp moved away for a few miles. Four days later my father went back to have one last look at her. When he came within two hundred yards, he saw someone sitting in front of the tipi.

It looked like my mother, but he thought it was a ghost. He stopped and was afraid to ride up to the tipi. He then decided to circle around the tipi at a safe distance. When he came in front of the tipi, mother saw him and stood up; at first he was going to ride away as fast as he could. But she yelled at him, and finally he came up to her. They then packed the tipi and went back to camp. Everyone thought she had died and came back to life again. I still believe this is what happened.

Zilda and Patrick Gunville

A Seven-Year Journey and the Life After

Zilda and Patrick Gunville

Patrick bought an automobile for $50, but I was afraid to ride in it, so he traded it for a house . . .

Zilda Delorme's parents, Chippewa and "a little French," came to the Pembina area from the woods west of Lake Superior sometime in the 1850s. Zilda was born in a wigwam near Pembina in 1876. Her father was an expert maker of Red River carts. Her telling of her band's seven-year journey from Pembina into Wyoming and back to the Turtle Mountains is an exceptional account of Chippewa life and customs and testimony to the strength of oral tradition. Patrick Gunville was born on the banks of the Milk River (Montana) in 1878 to Eliza (Chippewa) and Anthony Gunville (Chippewa and "a little French"). Zilda tells the family story.

ON 1877 WHEN I WAS A YEAR OLD, a great many Indians left the Pembina area on a buffalo hunt to the west. A priest traveled with us to teach the children and instruct the Indians spiritually.

During the summer of 1877 when our band was in camp, my mother was making soap in a large iron kettle. I was sitting on the ground near the fire. The kettle fell over and spilled onto me, burning me very badly.

31

I did not walk for two years after that. One time an old man stopped at our camp. Seeing me in that condition, he told my father that I would never walk if they did not make me. So father had my two brothers take a hold of me on each side and have me stand up and try to move my legs. It took a long time, but finally I walked.

During the summer of 1878 our group continued to hunt buffalo. We went south toward Miles City on the banks of the Yellowstone River. The Sioux tribe of Indians were a great worry to the Chippewa and Crees, making trouble for us. Sometimes we had fights with the Sioux.

When someone died while we were traveling on the prairies, men took some poles and fastened them together with leather; the body was wrapped in a blanket with personal property and then fastened securely to the poles. Other poles were driven into the ground, and the body was placed on the poles and fastened there. It was then left on the prairie. If we were in the woods when someone died, the body was fastened securely up in a tree and left there. We believed that some day the body would rise and that it had to be free. After the priest started to travel with us, he taught us to bury the dead in graves.

We reached Miles City, Montana, in the fall of 1879, where the men built cabins on the bank of the Yellowstone River. They built a rock wall around the cabins so the Sioux could not surprise us. That winter my father freighted for the businessmen of Miles City. He used the two-wheel carts to haul freight in.

In the spring of 1880 our party went south into what is now Wyoming. Among the sagebrush were small reptiles that looked like a frog but had a tail, and they did not jump, but ran. We called them "doctors," as we believed that if a person who got hurt would place one of the doctors on the wound the person would get well.

The winter of 1880 our group built cabins along the bank of some river where there was plenty of wood. We did not see a white person until the summer of 1881 when we were back in Montana. We were traveling north, still hunting buffalo. We spent the winter of 1881 somewhere southwest of Great Falls, Montana. In the spring of 1882 we continued to travel northeast, reaching Great Falls. Our leaders decided to winter there. Father freighted again that winter.

One day some of the young men were out on the ice on the river. A couple of young white men were with them. They were throwing their caps up in the air shooting at them. When a little Indian boy came after a pail of water which his mother had sent him for, the gun of one of the white men went off and instantly killed the little boy. The father wanted to go after the white man and kill him, but the priest talked to him and made him realize that it was an accident and that, therefore, he had no right to kill the man. It was hard for us to understand that vengeance was in God's hands.

In the spring of 1883 we left Great Falls, going east. We spent that winter on the banks of Flat Creek. One night during that winter the Sioux stole all of our horses, leaving us without any means of travel. Before we could go on in the spring, we had to trade buffalo hides and meat for horses. After we had enough horses we started on east. This was in the spring of 1884. I was eight years old. When we were near Terry, we saw a train for the first time. We were scared as we could not imagine what it was. Then the whistle blew, and we started to run across the prairie. We found out later that it was a train.

We crossed the Missouri River in Montana and took the same trail east. Instead of going on to Pembina, we went to Belcourt in 1884. Father settled on what he thought was reservation land and did not find out until 1894 that he had settled on land just west of the reservation boundary.

Our house was made of logs from the Turtle Mountains. After the house was finished, father started hauling freight from Devils Lake to the agency at Belcourt with two-wheel carts and horses. The old trail that he followed went south from Belcourt to Island Lake where there was a small settlement of cabins and dugouts. Then it went on to Wild Bill's cabin on Wolf Creek, twenty miles south of Island Lake; then twenty-five miles farther on was the next stop at Hurricane Lake, and then came Churches Ferry which was the last stop before reaching Devils Lake. It took about a week to make a trip. On the first trip father purchased windows for our house. The freight that he hauled was packed in wooden boxes. After the groceries and clothing were unloaded, some of the boxes were given to him to make the door for our house.

A Seven-Year Journey and the Life After

Belcourt was started in 1884 with the creation of the reservation. One hundred and thirty acres of it is government land. The agency and trading post stand on this land. The rest of the village is built around the agency and is partly leased government land and partly privately owned land. There was no railroad, so freight was hauled in. The agent was a man by the name of John Wells.

The Mission school at Belcourt was started by the Sisters of Mercy and Father Malo in 1885. The building was twenty-four by twenty-four feet, and it was built of logs. The school was in the charge of Mother Genevieve, Sister Anthone, Sister Mary, and Sister Angelica. I and my sisters and brothers were placed in the school in the fall of 1885.

Little Shell was the name of the Indian chief at this time. Father did not have a plow to break up his land, so he traded a large tent made of buffalo hides to Chief Little Shell for the use of his oxen and plow. In the spring of 1885 he broke up three acres of land and planted part of it to potatoes, corn, and wheat. He planted the wheat by hand, and in the fall he cut it with a grass hook and gathered it up by hand. To thresh it he put the wheat on a large piece of canvas and beat it with two sticks; then he lifted the grain up in his hands and let it fall slowly to the ground, letting the wind blow the straw and chaff out. The wheat was kept for chicken feed and for seed the next year.

In the winter father would haul wood from the Turtle Mountains to his farm. The pioneers living out on the prairie would come from many miles away and buy the wood from him. In the summer he continued to haul freight from Devils Lake to Belcourt.

In 1890 the school at Belcourt was not large enough to accommodate the children on the reservation, so the school was enlarged. One day while the children were out on the playgrounds, one of the scaffolds broke, so the carpenter, a Mr. Danielson, fell and was very badly hurt. The sisters at the school gave him a room at the school, and his son came and nursed him. Mr. Danielson was always a cripple after that.

About this time Mother Genevieve filed on a piece of land in Maryville Township. She sent some of the boys that were attending school to build a house on her homestead and to plow and seed the land for her.

One summer the gophers were eating the grain, so she took me and three other girls to help her put out poison. She made a stiff bread dough. We would pinch off a small piece of dough and dip it into the poison and then drop the dough by the gopher hole. Mother Genevieve later started the Catholic hospital in Devils Lake.

Our family had been attending church at the Belcourt mission. It was a long way to go, so the leaders decided to build a church in the country. Father had charge of the work as he was a good carpenter. The church was built west of his place of logs and had eight windows and two doors. Father Collins was in charge. The church was called Samshell, but later the name was changed to St. Michael.

When in 1894 father found out that his farm was not on the reservation, we could not go to the school at Belcourt any longer. He sent me and three of the other children to Fort Totten to attend school. I remained there at school until the spring of 1897. I came home that year and met a young man by the name of Patrick Gunville from St. John, and we became engaged to be married.

Patrick Gunville was born on August 30, 1877, on the banks of the Milk River in Montana. His parents were part Indian and part French. When General Miles gathered the Indians together at Fort Peck, Montana, in 1878, his parents were among them. They did not have far to go from their home on the Milk River. After the Indians were separated, the Canadians being sent back to Canada, Mr. and Mrs. Anthony Gunville did not return to their home. They traveled east into Dakota Territory. Another family by the name of Charles Patinaude went with them. They traveled in the two-wheel carts with horses, and then some of them rode on horses. They hunted buffalo and made pemmican, dried meat, and tanned hides as they went across the country. They reached a place in what is now Rolette County where there was a store about one mile south of the Canadian boundary line. This store was known as Wakapa, which is Chippewa meaning river. Mr. Gunville built a log cabin about two miles south of this store.

Patrick's father hauled freight from Grafton to St. John with two-wheel carts. The trail went south to Island Lake settlement and then east, just north of where Bisbee and Egeland now are, and then it went southeast across the country until Grafton was reached. These trips took a long time and were hard to make. Later on he hauled freight from Devils Lake, taking the same trail as my father traveled.

A Seven-Year Journey and the Life After

Indians traveling from Pembina, North Dakota to Fort Totten, North Dakota: Gathering Senega Root or Snakeroot
Photographed about 1910, families travel with horses and carts to gather the cash crop that brought fifteen to twenty cents a pound in the early 1900s.

For about two months each summer Mr. Gunville took his family and went picking buffalo bones. They would go south by Island Lake settlement and then to the place where the city of Leeds is now located. Then they went on to Minnewaukan, which is an Indian name meaning "bitter water" [liquor]. At that time there was only a store and a saloon at Minnewaukan. They sold the bones that they had picked up for six dollars per ton. The steamship came from Devils Lake to Minnewaukan after the bones that were brought there by the Indians. From Minnewaukan Mr. Gunville went southwest to a place they called Butte Marrail, meaning "big hill," and then to where the city of Harvey is now located. Then he went back northeast to a place known as Dogs Den, which was just a saloon out on the prairie, and then he went back to Minnewaukan where he again sold the bones which had been picked up. Devils Lake was then known as Creel Lake. They went back to St. John, taking a load of freight with them.

Between 1882 and 1884 Father Malo, a missionary priest from Manitoba, conducted the St. Cloude Mission north of St. John.

The school building was made of logs, and the roof was of clay. The only furniture was homemade long benches on which the children sat. There were no desks. The first, second, third and fourth grades were taught, and the old *Harpers Reader* was used. My husband Patrick and his brothers and sisters attended this school.

Zilda and Patrick Gunville

Patrick went to school for a few years, and then he worked with his father for a few years, after which he started out for himself. He was working for my father in the year of 1897 when I came home from the Fort Totten Indian School.

Patrick and I were married on January 24, 1898, at St. Michael Church by Father Malo. We lived with my parents for a while, then we moved to St. John, where Patrick worked at common labor in the winter. During the summers we would go out on the prairie digging snake root. We would travel in a wagon with horses and live in tents when digging the roots. At first we would wash the roots to get all of the dirt off. Then we were told not to wash the roots, as the washing took out the strength. We received from fifteen to twenty cents per pound for the roots. We would go east from St. John to Rock Lake, and as far east as Langdon. Our first child, a son, was born in 1901 and died in 1902. A daughter was born in 1903 and died the same year.

In 1905 we moved to the Turtle Mountain Reservation where another daughter was born and died in a few days. Then we bought a house and three lots in Dunseith and moved there where my husband worked at any kind of work he could get.

On May 21, 1909 our daughter, Rose, was born. She was the first child to live. In 1911 another daughter was born but died in just a few days.

We went to Bismarck, traveling in a covered wagon with horses. When we arrived Patrick obtained work on a freight boat owned by I.P. Baker. It went north to Washburn from Bismarck and south to a place called Forty-Eight.

Once when they were making a trip down the river, they got stuck on a sandbar in the middle of the river. They could not get off and were there for three days. Then one night while they were all asleep, the wind came up and the water rose, so they were released. The captain called the men but before they could get control of the boat, it ran into the bank, and they were nearly covered with dirt. They succeeded in getting the boat away from the bank just as a lot more dirt fell which would have completely covered them.

After that trip my husband worked on Bismarck's sewer.

A Seven-Year Journey and the Life After

Early in the spring of 1913 we and little daughter Rose left Bismarck in our covered wagon. We went south to Little Eagle, South Dakota, where we visited for a while. Then we went on to Thunder Butte where my husband worked for some Indians, helping to put up hay. For his work he received a horse and colt. Then we started back north. One night the horse, which we had worked for, got loose and went back to his former owner. My husband rode another horse and went after it. As he was riding along, his horse stopped so quickly that he nearly fell off. His horse would not go on, so Patrick looked to see what was the matter. He discovered there was a large rattlesnake in the road and had to ride around the snake. He found the strayed horse back at its old home. He took his horse and went back to the wagon. We arrived back in Dunseith, North Dakota, early in the fall of 1913.

In the fall of 1913 we bought a quarter-section of land at Bannerman, Manitoba, from the Canadian Pacific Railroad. We paid $11 per acre for it. We built a five-room house of logs, two rooms downstairs and three rooms upstairs. We had seven head of cattle and five head of horses. In the winter we lived in the house, but in the summer Patrick worked away from home so then we lived in the tent. One summer Patrick was helping build a house at Wakapa, Manitoba, so we were living in the tent. I heard a noise, looked around, and saw a big bull snake in the tent. I grabbed my little girl and ran out of the tent and over to the place where my husband was working. He went to the tent and killed the snake. We could not pay for the land, so we let it go back to the railroad.

In 1919 we went back to Dunseith. During the time we had been gone our house in Dunseith had burned down, so we had to rent a house. Patrick obtained work at the State Sanatorium.

Patrick bought an automobile for $50, but I was afraid to ride in it, so he traded it for a house and three lots without having to pay anything extra.

Martin Iron Bull

A Family of Yanktonai Medicine Men

Martin Iron Bull

I was taught to only believe in the Great Spirit.

A Yanktonai, Martin Iron Bull was born while his band was hunting in Montana in 1875. His grandfather, Boat Lip, and his father, Iron Bull, were both medicine men. Martin and his brother, Four Swords, were trained to be medicine men and in their turn became medicine men. Martin successfully farmed and raised cattle on the Standing Rock Reservation. He came to own twenty-six quarters of land, most of which he leased to white people.

MY GRANDFATHER, BOAT LIP, died in Montana about 1879. He was one hundred years of age and had been a medicine man for over fifty years. At the time of his death he was stooped and could not sit or stand erect. His hair was long and white, and his eyesight was gone. He knew his time was short so he called his friends and relatives to him and told them he was going away but would not die and for them not to cry when he was gone. He told them he would be living on a nearby hill. At this time the weather was cloudy and rainy. He told his friends he would leave them the first day the sun shone. A few days later the sun came out. Boat Lip asked to be placed in a round frame willow enclosure. The top was left uncovered, and the sun shone down upon him. Boat Lip said he would leave as the sun went down. He carried out his promise.

Grandfather had five wives and many children. He had a separate tipi for each wife.

He had become a medicine man because he had visions and could talk with the Great Spirit. He was good, kind, and gentle. He made medicine for the warriors, the hunters, and the sick and wounded. To help him make medicine, he used a stuffed skunk, badger, and a small coyote; a necklace made of shells, claws, stones, and pieces of hooves; and a pipe.

Grandfather taught my father, Iron Bull, in the ways of a medicine man, and on grandfather's death father became medicine man of the tribe. He died at the age of eighty-seven, and my brother, Henry Four Swords, became medicine man. Four Swords died in 1925, and I became the medicine man.

There were about 300 tipis in our camp. Each family had five to ten children. During the summer the children wore a skin breech cloth and moccasins. They spent most of the time playing, swimming, and riding. The Indian children did about as they pleased.

During the summer we followed the buffalo trail. We moved into the woods near a stream. During the winter we lived on dried meat, roots, and dried wild fruit. There was very little sickness among our people. We were strong and healthy, and most of us lived eighty to ninety years. In the winter months we wore only moccasins, breech cloth, mittens, and a skin cap. On the coldest days a buffalo robe was thrown over the shoulders. It became very cold in the tents as soon as the fire died down. In the morning we washed our faces and hands in the snow.

When I was six years old, my parents moved to the Cannon Ball Substation on the Standing Rock Reservation. Father, as medicine man, treated the sick. He encouraged the people to obey the government and help each other.

I started school at the Substation but had to quit because of my eyesight. During my boyhood around Cannon Ball, I spent my time playing, herding and watering horses, and taking long walks in the woods along the Missouri River. I and my older brother Henry Four Swords were trained to be medicine men by father. The training consisted of learning prayers and songs for the Great Spirit. As the prayers were said we faced the west holding a large pipe, then faced the south, east and north in turn and then touched the ground last. We were also taught to make medicine from roots and herbs.

At that time most of the Indians who were sick went to father to be cured. They believed in him and went to him in preference to the white doctor in Fort Yates. I was taught to only believe in the Great Spirit. I never attended a white man's church.

When I was nineteen years old, I worked for A.C. Wells, agent, at the Cannon Ball Substation. I ran errands and issued rations. I worked there for six years then moved twenty miles west of the Cannon Ball substation. I lived there for ten years and made my living raising cattle and horses. Then I moved back to Cannon Ball Substation and built a log cabin on my wife's land. Here I continued raising cattle.

From 1915 to 1926, I lived on the farm and worked at various periods in E.F. Underhill's store and pool hall. When my brother died in 1925, I then became the medicine man. I have been treating sick Indians who come to me ever since. In treating someone, I sing and say prayers to the Great Spirit and give them a dose of herbal medicine. If I am called, I will go to the sick Indian's home and administer to him. In some cases I have the person take a steam bath. In front of my house is a round willow framework about seven feet in diameter and three feet high. This is covered with two or three layers of canvas. In the center of this bath house is a round iron pan about two feet in diameter and eight inches deep. This is placed in the ground, the top of the pan being even with the ground. Stones about six inches in diameter are heated in an open campfire and when hot are carried into the bath house and placed in the pan. Cold water is poured on the rocks. This makes a steam that fills the bath house.

Over One Hundred Years on the Plains

Over One Hundred Years on the Plains

Louis Lafontaine

This was our land. There were no lines anywhere. There were no white men.

Born in 1829, Louis Lafontaine, a Chippewa, was well over one hundred years old when he was interviewed in the late 1930s — a life spanning American history from Andrew Jackson to Franklin D. Roosevelt. He hunted the wide-open northern plains, saw his mother killed by a Sioux, was caught up in the Riel Rebellion, and ended up in a small cabin on the tiny Turtle Mountain Reservation where he eked out a living.

MY MOTHER WAS KILLED BY THE SIOUX ABOUT 1847. A party of six tipis of Chippewa comprising ten or twelve families and at least twice that many men were hunting buffalo by Lake River in Dakota Territory. One day three of the men, unarmed, went out to look for wood. They were surprised by the Sioux who killed and scalped them. About fifty Sioux on foot attacked the camp. Of the Chippewa killed were three men and one woman, my mother. The women and children hid in the brush. We had flintlock guns. I had such a gun. At the critical moment the passage from the flintlock to the powder became plugged. I sneaked over to my mother, who was in the brush, to get a pin with which to open the hole. When I had done that and was ready to shoot, I stood up. A Sioux shot at me, and the bullet went between my legs and struck mother and killed her. If I had not stood up, probably my mother would not have been killed. I shot three Sioux and think that

Louis Lafontaine

I got the one who killed my mother. I wanted to scalp them, but father would not allow it, as we had become Catholics. The fight started in the forenoon and lasted until dusk at which time the Sioux left.

In my youth and middle age there were no lines between either the states or territories or the United States and Canada. This was our land. There were no lines anywhere. There were no white men. We hunted the buffalo, had enough to eat, and were satisfied. Lines were being surveyed, however, before I came to Rolette County. I saw a party of surveyors in Canada running a line that appeared to go from Winnipeg to Lake Manitoba. The surveyors had a camp near St. Boniface. They made about twenty-five miles a day using a wheel to measure the distances.

In my youth I saw Crow Indians shoot buffalo with bows and arrows. Flintlock guns were common. Later muzzle-loading cap guns came into use. I was along on many buffalo hunts and have killed over three thousand of the animals. When I was about forty years old, I shot fifty buffalo in one day on one hunt. I then had a repeating rifle. That would be in about 1868 or 1869. I did most of my buffalo hunting on the Milk River in Montana. On one buffalo hunt at Oak Lake in Manitoba, I got lost in a blizzard. The storm raged for many days. I had a wigwam along, so I had shelter, but I ran out of food and had nothing to eat for six days. When I finally succeeded in getting home, I was so weak that I just wobbled along. My people wintered in Canada that year.

About two years before my mother died, my people were in trouble with the Sioux. A band of Chippewa were then camping at Dog Den south of present-day Towner. The band split up into two camps, one large and one small. The smaller camp consisted of three tipis. A party of Sioux on horseback and on foot attacked the smaller camp. There were said to be about eight thousand Sioux in camp not far away. The fight between the small number of Chippewa and the Sioux continued for two days. The men in the other camp heard the shooting and came to the rescue. When they came, the Sioux abandoned the attack. One Chippewa and a large number of Sioux were killed. During the night, the Sioux withdrew. When the bodies of the fallen Sioux were "dipped" in a nearby lake, the water turned red.

Over One Hundred Years on the Plains

I saw Sitting Bull in Montana and Louis Riel in Montana and in Canada. In fact, I took part in the Riel Rebellion. Indians from Canada went down to Montana to get Riel to come up there and be their leader. They held many meetings at which they discussed the situation. They planned on sending Riel to the Queen to lay the Indians' trouble before her. The complaint of the Indians was that they had not been served right. When the trouble started, there was lots of snow. When it was over, the leaves were big. During the spring and early summer, there was only fighting once in a while. When a body of soldiers first met Riel with his Indians, Riel went out to meet the soldiers with a cross in his hands. When he came near to the soldiers, he kneeled down and raised the cross. The soldiers fired and shot the cross out of his hand. That ended the meeting for that day. The next day the fight was on for good. An army came from Regina to reinforce the Canadian force already on the spot. Many were killed on both sides, in all about sixty Indians. When the Indians ran out of ammunition, Riel gave himself up. The Canadian soldiers roamed over the district setting fire to the houses and shooting horses and cattle. I had three hundred dollars in my house when it was burned.

With nothing left, I went to the Indian agency at Crooked Lake, Saskatchewan, but was told that I did not belong there. The agent sent me away. Then I came back to the United States. I went to Chief Little Shell and asked permission to stay in the Turtle Mountains. The first year I was at Turtle Mountain, I built a log cabin, which I plastered with clay and covered with a roof of poles, hay, and sod. It was about twelve feet long and fourteen feet wide with a door to the east and two half-windows, one to the south and one to the north. I split logs for the floor. For light I used a rag dipped in grease at first and later kerosene. Of split logs, I made a table, benches, shelves, and bunks. I had no stove but used an open chimney. There was wood right on the land. Groceries were obtained from the supplies stored by the government at Belcourt. I obtained water from a slough and did not dig a well until several years later. My first crop was potatoes. I broke up the sod with a hatchet. I took an old ax head and put on a handle to make a hoe-like affair.

Adjustment to the Reservation

Robert Little Bird

The Indians did not make good farmers.

Little Bird, a Yankton Sioux, was born on the east side of the Missouri River across from Fort Yates in 1872. The Yankton camp consisted of 260 lodges of between two and eight persons per lodge. Two Bears, Red Fish, Iron Thunder, and Big Head were the chiefs. Little Bird belonged to the Cuthead Band of which Big Head was the chief. His story relates the difficult adjustment from the free life on the plains to the confinement of the reservation.

OUR YANKTON BANDS WERE ALL FRIENDLY WITH THE WHITE PEOPLE. Our hunting grounds were located east from the Missouri River to Minnesota and from Canada south into what is now the state of South Dakota.

During the summer months we hunted over this area. The hunters killed deer, antelope, rabbits, and coyotes with bow and arrows. There were very few buffalo on the east side of the Missouri River at this time. Buffalo were to be found two hundred miles west of the Missouri River, so the hunters went there occasionally. We used a travois to pull our possessions when on the march. The travois consisted of two tent poles tied up over the horse's neck; the other end of the poles dragged on the ground. A round hoop, made of willows and crisscrossed strips of hides, was tied on the poles. The tents and clothing were tied on the round

Adjustment to the Reservation

Beef Ration Day at Standing Rock Reservation
Adapted from a photograph by D.F. Barry in the 1880s (SHSND C0844).

framework. Babies rode on the travois and also older children when they became tired.

In 1876 we received orders from the government that we would have to give up our hunting lands and live on the Standing Rock Reservation. We then moved to Fort Yates, Dakota Territory, for two years. From the agency we received rations consisting of beef, bacon, flour, syrup, sugar, salt pork, lard, and baking powder.

In 1878 the Cuthead Band moved from Fort Yates to the Cannon Ball agency because there was better hunting there. We received rations once a week at Cannon Ball. The cattle were slaughtered by the Indians and divided by the chiefs.

After moving to the Cannon Ball Agency, we continued living in our tipis. During the summer months we camped on the prairies, while in the winter we camped near the Missouri. The tipis were pitched in a circle. A fence made of poles and willows was built around the camp. When I was a boy, I spent most of my time playing with a bow and arrows. I had one in my hands just about all the time. My father, First Hail, made the bow and arrows for me. I was sixteen years old when I started going to the subagency school at Cannon Ball. I learned to talk a little English, write, and figure. I did not care much for school. I spent most of my time hunting along the Missouri and Cannonball rivers. I hunted with Jerome Cotton Wood and for White Lightning. We hit a deer or antelope at fifty yards with bow and arrows just about every time. If we wounded a deer or antelope, we kept after it until we killed it. I have chased a wounded antelope as far as forty miles before finally killing it.

In 1888 the government wanted us to quit living in tipis and to build log houses. Up to this time we were healthy and strong, but after that many became sick and weak. The agent gave each Indian a plow, seed, a scythe, a cow, wagon, and a team of horses if he would build a log cabin and farm the land. We planted corn, beans, potatoes, onions, and squash. My father did not like farming so my mother and I did all of the work. We did not milk our cow, and we could not kill it either. Many of the Indians said they lost their cows, but these were all butchered and eaten. The hide was buried in the ground so the agent or Indian policemen could not find it.

The Indians did not make good farmers, so in 1890 or 1891 the government gave each Indian family five to ten head of cattle. When I reached the age of twenty-one, the government gave me five cows. My brand was number 22. I branded my cows and turned them loose on the prairie. All of us let our cattle graze on the prairies. It was just one big ranch from Cannon Ball to Fort Yates. We had a roundup about the first of July and branded our calves. We all sold a few cows to the government agency at Fort Yates every year. When we made a sale, we received a check for the full amount.

We got along nicely from 1895 to 1915. All the Indians had cattle and horses. After the reservation was opened up to white people in 1915, the government and the white people soon forced us out of the cattle business. The government encouraged us to lease or sell our land to the white people. After we sold or leased our land, most of us sold our cattle and horses. We no longer did any work, and hard times came upon us.

Hunting Buffalo and Fighting Blackfeet

Hunting Buffalo and Fighting Blackfeet

Many Horses

Chasing Bear fell over dead and Shoots Close was wounded in the leg.

Many Horses was born in 1858 when his camp, about one thousand Lakota, was located near present-day New Salem. His father had earned a reputation as an excellent horse raider, mostly from the Crow, Pawnee, and Blackfeet. Because he had captured so many horses for his people, he named his son Many Horses. His recollection describes the Lakota method of buffalo hunting and his experience as a warrior against the Blackfeet.

I SPENT MY BOYHOOD PLAYING WAR AND HUNTING GAMES. The boys did whatever they wanted to, but the girls had to help their mothers.

I was about fifteen years old when the tribe moved to Montana. The buffalo had changed their course, and we had to move with the buffalo.

In hunting the buffalo, scouts were sent out to locate them. They would then come back and tell the camp what they had found. The chiefs then gave orders for the camp to move.

In the camp were many Indians with their faces painted with grease and charcoal. They kept order and carried out the chiefs' orders. They used clubs and would kill if one resisted. On moving camp to the hunting grounds, orders were given for everyone to be quiet; the dogs were tied up and no one was to fire a gun. Game could be killed only with bow and arrow while we were on the march. When we arrived within a few miles of the buffalo, camp was made.

The hunters went out on their fastest horses. A few of the hunters had guns, but most of them used bow and arrows. Some of the older Indians came after them on pack horses to carry the meat back to camp.

The hunters would try to keep out of sight of the buffalo until they were close to them. This they did by keeping behind the hills and sometimes waiting until the buffalo came near them. The hunters on the best horses rode out into the buffalo herd and scattered them in all directions. The others then rushed out and took after the buffalo. They tried to kill only the young fat ones.

A few could kill a buffalo with one arrow, but usually it took two or more arrows. The buffalo ran two or three hundred yards after being shot. Each hunter had a mark on his arrows so he could tell which buffalo were his. Sometimes the arrow would break off when the buffalo fell, and one of the hunters would stick one of his arrows into the wound. The hunters then argued about whose buffalo it was, and sometimes got into fights. On these hunts they usually killed about fifty or sixty buffalo. The hunter that killed the buffalo got the hide and first choice of one-third of the meat. The rest of the meat was divided among the other Indians.

July was the most dangerous month in which to hunt buffalo. The bulls guarded the cows and attacked horse and rider, killing many horses and sometimes even the rider.

I was about eighteen years of age when I killed my first buffalo with bow and arrow. Some of the hunters could kill ten or twelve buffalo in one day. My record was seven killed with bow and arrow.

Everyone had plenty to eat, living mainly on fresh and dried buffalo meat. The women gathered wild berries, onions, and turnips.

The camp moved from place to place as the buffalo moved. The buffalo looked for new feeding grounds, and their course was also changed by the hunters.

It was dangerous to go hunting alone as one was apt to run into roving bands of Crow, Pawnee, and Blackfeet Indians.

Hunting Buffalo and Fighting Blackfeet

I was about twenty years of age when I went on the warpath. I and eleven other young warriors went out on foot, looking for trouble. We were armed with rifles and knives. We had been gone two days and had not seen any enemy Indians, so we decided to camp in a ravine during the night. It was just beginning to get dark. We were sitting on some rocks and eating a cold lunch. We did not think there was an enemy within a hundred miles of us. All at once shots rang out. Chasing Bear fell over dead, and Shoots Close was wounded in the leg. I and the others lay down behind the rocks for protection. I had seen some of the other Indians and knew we were attacked by Blackfeet. The Blackfeet were in the rocks higher up on the hillside, and I could not tell how many there were. Everyone was shooting and pieces of rock were flying in the air. One more of us Sioux was killed, and two more were wounded. I thought we had killed one or two Blackfeet. I thought we were outnumbered and would not be able to escape. The firing kept up until dark, and then both sides stopped. It became very quiet. We did not know if the Blackfeet were sneaking down on us or not. We then decided to fight our way out. With knives in one hand and a gun in the other, we slowly made our way up the hill. We did not run into any of the enemy, so we hurried away.

About twenty years later, we Indians from different tribes would sometimes get together and talk over different fights. In this way I got to know some of the Blackfeet who had been in the fight. I found out that there had been twenty-five Blackfeet in the fight and that they had left as soon as it got dark.

In the evenings the men sat around the fires, held councils, and told stories. The peace pipe was passed around. Each man took four puffs and passed the pipe on. After smoking the peace pipe, they could not tell a lie.

We had few laws, but the ones we did have were obeyed. I cannot understand the white man's law. They make laws and then break them and also taught the Indians how to break them.

Ouiskin and Wanapi

Farming near Pembina and in the Turtle Mountains

*Ouiskin and Wanapi
Rising Sun and Lone Child*

Seven other children were born to us, but they all died as babies.

Rising Sun (b. 1815) and Lone Child (b. 1820) were among the few Pembina-area Chippewa who in the 1860s and 1870s did not take part in the buffalo hunts. They made their living by farming. Rising Sun worked during the winters, first for the Hudson's Bay Company carrying supplies by dogsled from Hudson's Bay to Pembina, and later for the American Fur Company carrying furs and goods to and from St. Paul by dogsled. He was one of the first to settle permanently in the Turtle Mountains.

In 1861 Lone Child gave birth to Ouiskin in a wigwam near the Pembina settlement. Ouiskin tells the family's story.

MY PARENTS DID NOT TRAVEL WITH THE BAND on buffalo hunts but remained near Pembina. They did not have land of their own but just lived on someone else's. They raised lots of corn, potatoes, and vegetables which they took to Pembina to trade for meat and things that they needed.

For a long time they dug the ground with sticks, but after a few years they had a walking plow. My mother and I did most of the planting and

Farming near Pembina and in the Turtle Mountains

A Traditional Chippewa Couple
*The name "Rising Sun" is common among the Chippewa.
This man and woman from the Turtle Mountains were named
Rising Sun and Simaquam (SHSND A6767).*

took care of the crop through the summer. Father purchased a mower so after that it was not so hard to cut the hay for our oxen and horses.

In the spring of 1882 father decided that he wanted land of his own. He sold everything that would not fit in two Red River carts and moved to the Turtle Mountains. I and my five brothers and sisters, of course, went along.

Although I was twenty-one years old, I had never traveled more than a few miles from home before. We camped along the way and cooked on campfires. We traveled southwest, passing south of Rock Lake, and then on west until we came to a place where there was just one building at the foot of the mountains. This building was the beginning of Dunseith.

We went northeast of Dunseith about two and one-half miles. We set up our wigwam and remained there about one month. Father was allotted land two miles west of where we had settled, so we moved our wigwam to this land to live in while the house was being built. We had never lived in a house.

Father thought that he would build a large house. He and my brothers cut down oak trees on his land. The main part of the house was thirty by sixteen feet, divided into three rooms, and a large lean-to was built onto the side. Each room had a large window in it. The door was made of oak planks which had been split and smoothed off with an axe. The floor was made of the same kind of planks. Father had dug a large cellar, but it was not walled up. Oak poles were split and laid close together for the roof, and then hay and sod were placed on top. A fireplace was built in the large part of the house.

When father got that far with the building of the house, he needed windows and hinges and some other things, so he and one of my brothers took one of the carts and the pony and went back to Pembina to purchase the things they wanted. They also brought a cast-iron cookstove back with them. Father cut hay with the mower that summer, raked it up by hand, and hauled it in the carts and stacked it.

That winter it was hard for us as we had been accustomed to raising potatoes, corn, and vegetables. Now we had to depend on meat from deer and elk of which there were many and on fish which we caught in the lakes.

There was a nice spring at the boot of the hill, where the house was located, so that we did not have to dig a well. We had homemade furniture of poles and split planks.

In the spring of 1883 father and the boys spaded up ground and planted corn, potatoes, and a garden for other vegetables. Mother, I, and the girls did the planting and took care of it.

That summer we picked berries and dried them in the Indian manner for winter. We also dried corn when it was ready. When we made pemmican, we added some of the corn to the meat.

In the spring and summer of 1883 white people came to the place at the foot of the mountain where the one building was standing and started to put up other buildings. The Indians called it the Ouiskin

Farming near Pembina and in the Turtle Mountains

settlement. We were soon going there and trading furs and hides and also moccasins for tea, tobacco, and other things that we wanted.

In the spring of 1884 father had a much larger piece of ground ready to plant to corn.

Mother and we girls made all of our clothes. Most of the garments were made of the hides of buffalo, and then later from deer and elk. It was not long until we did not have any hides with which to make clothes. We then started to purchase clothes that were ready-made. Only our moccasins were made from animal hides.

My parents never sent us children to school, and we did not receive any religious instruction.

About 1885 or 1886 an Indian by the name of Wanapi came to the Turtle Mountains from the west, and he settled on land northeast of Dunseith.

Wanapi was born at Rocky Boy, Montana, in 1854. His parents were Raining Thunder and All Day Bright Sun. They were traveling with other Indians hunting buffalo. In 1876 they were near present-day Williston where they had trouble with the Sioux Indians, and Raining Thunder was killed. Wanapi was then twenty-two years old. He and his mother continued to travel with the band until the buffalo became so scarce that they had to do something else for a living, so they came to the Turtle Mountains.

They traveled in a Red River cart with a pony. Where they purchased their land, they set up the wigwam to live in while they built their house. The next year Wanapi started farming. He only had a small plot the first year, but it was not long until he was farming most of his land.

In 1893 Wanapi and I were married according to the Indian custom. I went to Wanapi's home to live with him and his mother.

In February 1894 our first child, a son, was born. We named him Alfred. In 1901 another son was born, and we named him Fred. In 1910 our daughter, Alice, was born. Seven other children were born to us, but all died as babies.

Mandan and Hidatsa Ways

Sitting Crow
Poor Wolf

Sitting Crow was the grandson of the Mandan Chief, Red Cow.

When Poor Wolf was seventeen, he had smallpox — the scourge of 1837.

Charles L. Hall and his wife, Emma, arrived at Fort Berthold in 1876 to establish a Christian missionary station. Hall, educated in theology and architecture, built his mission outside of the fort and near Like-A-Fishhook Village where the Mandan, Hidatsa, and Sanish (Arikara) lived. He learned the native languages and in 1884 began a school. Because the WPA worker, unfortunately, for whatever reason, did not conduct interviews on the Fort Berthold Reservation, only the accounts of Sitting Crow and Poor Wolf, as told by Charles Hall, are in the Historical Data's pioneer biography files.

Sitting Crow's Story

PEDITSKA AMAKISH ("SITTING CROW") was born in 1861 at the old Fish-hook Village (Fort Berthold). The Mandans, the Hidatsa, and the Arikaras had come to live there together. At eight years of age, he was a little boy, hunting birds and gophers with a bow and arrows. Sitting Crow was a grandson of the Mandan chief Red

Mandan and Hidatsa Ways

Cow and a nephew of Ieenape, a son of the chief. So by birth he was in line for leadership of his tribe.

His uncle Ieenape, "One -who-turns-away-his-Face," was of a reticent habit, but though shy, had broken away from his Indian life and gone nine hundred miles down the Missouri River with General C. H. Howard and spent a year in the home of Dr. Alfred L. Riggs. He was not a Christian, but when the first missionaries came among his people in 1876, he was a friend and an interpreter.

Sitting Crow was at that time a boy of fifteen, but the attitude of his uncle, twenty years older, who still clung to his tribal inheritance, did not seem to have had any effect on the lad. He was a part of the life which Mandan boys had lived for hundreds of years. When he was sixteen, he took part in the Wapikeh, the Sun Dance, for he wanted not only to be like the other young men but to excel them as as a good fighter. They wanted to pass the tests that would give them repute as brave and patriotic. After fasting two days and nights hunger got the better of Sitting Crow for a time. Later he entered the arbor, made of posts and poles and green boughs, with a shaggy head of a buffalo on a high pole in the center. A dry buffalo skull was on a mound of dirt at the side of the entrance. Men daubed with white clay, with eagle feathers hanging down their backs, danced about. For three days and nights they had been sitting before their totems in the arbor without food or drink. Now they danced and blew whistles made of goose bones. A band of older men chanted to the rhythm of drum beats. Soon they had to rest, then they danced again. A leader danced back and forth between the head and the skull till he fell. Then he revived and danced again till he fell, again, revived and danced again till at last he lay in unconsciousness.

One of the dancers stepped out to the middle. It was Sitting Crow. An older man slit the flesh of his back, inserted a wooden skewer, tied a rawhide to the skewer and fastened the other end to the nostrils of the buffalo head. Sitting Crow danced, jerking at the cord, while men chanted and whistles blew. A crowd of men, women, and children watched from outside. He rushed in a circle and wound himself around the pole, howling and with eyes fixed on the buffalo head. He reversed and wound the other way. Then he fainted. Did he see a spirit which would give him success in hunting or fighting or driving away the evil spirits that caused sickness? Some believed that they saw a spirit embodied in some animal form, a bear, a hawk, an eagle or a snake, and get help to win honors and aid the tribe. Sitting Crow went away to sleep and to be fed soup when he awoke.

When he was eighteen years old, his father urged him to go and seek his protecting spirit on a hill across the Missouri River from the Indian village. Sitting Crow went in December, without food or drink for three days. He crawled into a hole in the side of the bluff, like a coyote. On the third night he fell into a sleep of exhaustion and was rewarded with a dream. A man came and gave him an eagle feather. Then he went home, wondering what the interpretation would be.

Some time after this an uncle who had gone to live with the Crow-Flies-High band of Hidatsas at Fort Buford, one hundred miles up the river, came to visit and Sitting Crow went back with him. While he was at Fort Buford, a roving band of Sioux drove off a bunch of the Hidatsas' horses, and Sitting Crow was with a party that chased the enemy. He succeeded in striking one of the Sioux with a stick which was more glory than killing with a shot at a distance.

Thus Sitting Crow earned his right to wear his first eagle feather, his "Croix-de-guerre" — his medal.

In 1884 when Sitting Crow was twenty-two, he went with a hunting party as far as the Powder River in Montana, more than three hundred miles away from the home village. There the members of the party found a large herd of buffalo and returned to camp with plenty of meat. Sitting Crow stayed behind, as he had again decided to drag a head. This time he was left alone in the dark. As he started along the beaten trail, his load grew heavy. Perhaps this trail was one the buffalo disliked, and their spirits made the burden heavy. He left the trail and went on the untracked prairie. The burden was still grievous. A storm came up. He dragged on, wailing as he went. He was lost. The storm passed. Dawn came. He climbed a hill and sighted the camp five miles away. He moistened the dried wound on his back with spittle. He got the rawhide cord untied. He set the buffalo head on the hill. He said to it, "We have spent the night together. Now I leave you, Sacred One. Some day you will help me and make me brave."

When he reached the camp, the people were eating; but his grandfather, the old chief Red Cow, was sleeping. The old man had spent the night keeping up a fire on the hill that his grandson might find the camp.

After this, Sitting Crow was again on a hunt when an angry bull turned and knocked down his horse. He escaped and the horse was only bruised, as the bull ran off with the herd. At another time in the melee, someone shot, and he felt a bullet whiz by. It had gone through the loose flapping end of his shirt. He felt that it was through dragging the head of a buffalo that twice he had been saved.

At another time, when Sitting Crow was with a war party chasing some Sioux who were driving off a bunch of horses, he recovered two of the horses. He thought that this success was given him by a spirit because he had dragged the head of a buffalo during a long night.

Poor Wolf

POOR WOLF WAS BORN in one of the five Hidatsa villages on the Knife River where it empties into the Missouri. His uncle, "Road Maker" (Adihidish), was a leader among his people when Lewis and Clark visited the villages in 1804-1805. Poor Wolf reckoned that he was born in 1820, and as a little boy remembered seeing white soldiers come up the river in eight wooden boats which they pulled with ropes from the bank. These whites made an agreement with Indians about their hunting grounds. The little boy recollected saying to his father (Buffalo-hide-tent), "Will I be a white man now?" His father said, "Yes." In old age, Poor Wolf looking back would say, "I have been a friend to the whites ever since."

When a child, only four years old, Poor Wolf prayed to animals and to the sun, moon, and stars. He was afraid of the enemy in the dark. Through a trader, his father had heard of the white man's Great Spirit, and in this way had some dim knowledge of God. He used to be afraid of the white man's teaching.

When Poor Wolf was seventeen, he had smallpox — the scourge of 1837 — and many of the people died. The others abandoned their villages and stayed away until three mysterious figures in black told them that it was safe to return. Poor Wolf was left alone, helpless, with swollen face and eyes half-closed. A bear came in and walked right to where he was, sat down with his back pressed against him and began to scratch his breast with its forepaws. By and by, he got up and walked out of the lodge. Then the bear came back and while Poor Wolf trembled with fear, went through the same motions again. The boy thought surely the bear had mercy on him, and when his father returned, they talked it over and agreed that the bear pitied him. After that, he worshiped the bear in the dance, wearing anklets of bear's teeth.

When the boy was nineteen or twenty, and still unmarried, he fasted for twenty days, going without food and not smoking for four days, on the fifth day eating a little and then fasting again. During this time he went about crying aloud, and after he ceased to fast, he still went about crying for a year. He would stand on a buffalo skull and cry until his throat was dry. At the end of this fast, his father cut four pieces from his upper arm and four from the lower arm, as a sacrifice to his gods. After these wounds were healed, the youth entered a lodge, where there were many old men, and, with great ceremony, they painted on his arms and all over one side of his breast and back. Two men did the work while the men would sing, "Let his body be pictured, his spirit also. O, White Father in heaven and ye four winds that make him blue. Let him not be bitten by rattlesnakes, etc." It was thought that he could not be struck by bullets from an enemy; that he could suck out poison without harm; that the tattooing would give him protection and make him courageous.

Recounting his history, the old man said, "Once a hundred warriors, out on a trip, became very hungry. I had a piece of buffalo meat concealed, which I carried along. This I roasted and gave to them, and they were saved from starving. In consequence one of the warriors, who had taken part in a Sun Dance, gave me the name of Poor Wolf." He had continued dancing for four days until all others stopped and then had kept on for another four days. In a dream he saw a wolf that told him he would have a long life. So he gave the name of Poor or Lean Wolf to the one who saved his life.

An eagle hunter was reckoned a man of distinction among the Indians. There was a bluff near the village where they used to worship when they went on expeditions. Poor Wolf once caught twelve eagles on

Mandan and Hidatsa Ways

one hunt, three in one day. There are very strict rules for hunting, but Poor Wolf did not observe them all. One rule was that the most successful hunter should return to the camp with his eagles, weeping. Poor Wolf came back happy. They prayed to the fiber rope with which they caught the eagles. Two leaders in an eagle hunt wear eagle feathers around their necks and sing songs in the night. Poor Wolf liked to go about the business in his own way and had an eagle claw tattooed on his right hand. His uncle put it on so he could grab a Sioux.

It is plain that Poor Wolf was a religious man as well as a political leader. He believed in the Great Spirit and greatly influenced his people, who in turn rewarded him for his spiritual services.

Poor Wolf
Born in the early 1820s, Poor Wolf lived to see the first automobiles arrive at Fort Berthold after his people moved there from Like-A-Fishhook (SHSND A0137-02)

Skylark Fly

On Lakota Life

Skylark Fly
(Charles Ramsey)

Next to the eagles, the coyotes were looked upon with reverence.

Skylark Fly was born at the Grand River agency in 1870. In 1872 his people were moved to Fort Yates. When he was six years old his parents insisted that he go to boarding school, which he attended until he was eighteen years old, learning harness repair and carpentry. While away at school, he was given the name Charles Ramsey, which he retained. He explains much about the Lakota way of life, about chiefs, warriors, the importance of eagles and coyotes, marriage, laws, and death.

ON 1888 I RETURNED TO FORT YATES where I was given work by the government repairing harnesses. I worked at this trade for two years and was doing this work at the time Sitting Bull was killed in 1890.

The night the policemen were sent out to arrest Sitting Bull, all government employees had orders to remain in the agency office, in case they should be needed. The first news we received of Sitting Bull's death was when Paints Brown, one of the policemen, rode in. Paints Brown had left the fight and came to Fort Yates to get more ammunition for the policemen. We were all very excited at the news. Major McLaughlin told them the soldiers would take care of the trouble at the Sitting Bull camp. When the dead policemen were brought in, I washed and dressed them and got them ready for burial.

I was next employed by the government to do carpenter work. I worked in Fort Yates and at the Porcupine Substation at Shields.

On Lakota Life

In 1894 my parents prevailed upon me to enter the government school at Hampton, Virginia. I attended this school for three years and enjoyed it very much. About half the students were Negroes. The Negroes and Indians did not like each other, but there was little trouble among them as they left each other alone. In addition to regular subjects, I learned the blacksmith trade.

In 1897 I returned to Fort Yates where I was employed by the government as a blacksmith. I worked there for three years and in 1900 was sent to the Porcupine Station at Shields where I had charge of the blacksmith shop for ten years.

I then moved on my allotment land near Big Lake (nine miles south of Cannon Ball) where I farmed and raised horses and cattle.

During the summer of 1879 when I was nine years old, many of the Indians, including my parents, in and around Fort Yates decided to go on a buffalo hunt. About one hundred and fifty Indians — men, women, and children and one Negro, Andrew Slater — went on the hunt. We traveled in wagons or on horseback southwestward in single file. At night we camped and were on our way early in the morning. On the third day out of Fort Yates a deer jumped up. Many shot at it with arrows but missed. Andrew Slater who was in the end of the line grabbed his rifle and shot at the deer. This made the Indians angry, and they gave Slater a bad beating with sticks. He had disregarded the orders about firing a gun while we were on the march. On the sixth day out we made camp, and the men got ready to hunt on the next day.

I liked this life and while the men were out hunting, I and the other children played on the hills or swam in a nearby stream.

The men hunted for three days, and enough buffalo were killed so that each family got one. About a week was spent in camp dressing and drying the meat on poles in the sun. Everyone ate all the meat he wanted, and nobody became sick.

We children liked this life out in the open. We were very sorry when the camp packed up and started on the journey back to Fort Yates.

The bravest man in the tribe was made a chief. He had killed more enemies, saved more lives, and stolen the most horses on raids than any of the others. The chief was given a large coat covered with shells, claws, and polished deer hooves. There were long fringes on the shoulders and arms. The chief had the largest tent, the best clothes, and the largest pipe. Horsehair dyed yellow and fastened to the pipe signified that it belonged to a chief.

The bottom and top of the chief's tent was colored black because he was victorious in battle. If the chief had been wounded in battle, a red stripe was painted around the tent.

In making laws and decisions the chief was aided by a council of old men. They used a council tent or met in the chief's tent. The peace pipe was passed around; after that whatever they said was the truth. As they sat around talking, they used a sharp pointed stick to scratch their heads. They had all killed enemies in battle, and they believed if they used their fingers to scratch themselves, they would lose their minds. The chief usually did as the council wished. The old men were thought to be very wise. After the meeting one of the old men was sent out to announce the decision of the chief and the council. He walked through the camp and talked as loudly as he could.

The young Indian braves were anxious to take part in a fight with an enemy so they could earn their feathers. If they killed an enemy, they were entitled to wear one white eagle feather. The first four that touched a dead or wounded enemy also were entitled to a white feather. They also received a white feather for saving the life of a friend who was in danger during the fight.

If a warrior was wounded, he could wear one red feather for each wound. If he was wounded with an arrow, the red feather was split down the center. Warriors could wear or use the feathers as they wished, but at no time could they use more feathers than they had earned. If their horse was killed in battle, they cut off the tail and dyed it red.

Eagles were usually hunted in the spring of the year. Anyone could hunt eagles. The eagles could only be killed with the bare hands, otherwise the hunter would have bad luck. A hole was dug on the top of a large hill. The hole was made just large enough for the hunter to sit down in. The top of the hole was then covered with sticks, grass, and dirt. On top of this, a dead rabbit was placed as bait. Sometimes a snare was placed around the bait so as to catch the eagle's legs when it would land near the bait. Other times the hunter reached up, grabbed the eagle by the legs, and pulled it down into the hole. As the hunter twisted the eagle's neck to kill it, he said a prayer. He called the eagle his grandfather and asked to be forgiven for killing the eagle. He was very sorry and cried real tears. To kill an eagle and not ask its forgiveness would bring bad luck. The hunter might lose his best horse or some member of his family might die.

After the eagle was killed, it was wrapped in sage leaves for three days. The feathers were then pulled out. The white feathers with a black tip were the most valuable. The eagle was skinned, but the flesh was not eaten. Some of the bones were used to make whistles. The claws were dried and made into ornaments. We Indians revered the eagle.

Next to the eagles, the coyotes were revered. The coyote could be killed in any manner. The hunter had to ask the coyote for forgiveness when he killed it or it would bring bad luck to him or his family. The skin of the coyote was painted different colors and was used as a good luck charm. It only brought good luck to the Indians of the best character.

At night when the coyotes howled, the Indians could tell from the tone what the weather would be and also what kind of hunting they might expect in the next few days.

The people had few laws. They did not need laws because most of them were honest and good. Their conscience told them what was right and what was wrong. They were good to each other, and there were few quarrels.

In each camp was a group of men appointed by the chief to keep order and see that his orders were carried out. These men were of good character and were not hotheaded. In case someone broke one of the chief's commandments, these men would catch the offender and whip him or beat him with clubs. They might break his gun or bow and arrows or slash his tipi to pieces with knives. The offender was not given any kind of trial.

In case of an unprovoked murder, the murderer was driven from the camp and became an outcast and had to live alone with his conscience. In about a year's time, he could come back to camp. Nothing was done to protect the murderer from the relatives of the murdered person. If the murder was justified, the man was given protection from the relatives of the murdered person. The peace pipe was smoked and every effort was made to settle the trouble.

Skylark Fly

If a man wanted a girl, he began his courtship by giving presents to her and her family. He then asked the father for the girl. The father usually took his time in saying "yes" as the longer he put off giving his girl away, the more presents he would get. The presents consisted of horses, weapons, or clothing. If the father liked the man and did not have anything against the man's relatives, he let the girl go. There was no marriage ceremony. The man took the girl, and they lived with his parents until he was given a tipi or built one for himself. The best warriors could have as many wives as they could support. It was considered an honor to give a daughter to one of the warriors.

The dead were buried on scaffolds made of poles or in the trees. The bodies were wrapped in hides along with some cherished possessions. The bodies were lashed on the scaffolds so the wind could not blow them off. There was no burial ceremony, and the body was prepared for burial as soon as possible. Everyone in the camp went to the tipi to see the dead person. It was their privilege to take anything in the tipi they wanted. This showed the affection the relatives had for the departed one.

Traditional Burial Scaffold
Photographed in 1882 (SHSND 0119-07).

On Lakota Life

In case a warrior was killed in battle, his body was brought back to camp if possible. If his fellow warriors could get the body but could not get it back to camp, they buried it under a pile of rocks. The dead warrior may have told his best friend that in case he was killed in battle, he wanted his horse killed and placed beside him, or that the friend could have the horse for himself. The Indians visited the graves occasionally and kept them in good repair.

The dead were buried any place near the camp. Only one body was placed on a scaffold unless it happened that four or five were killed in battle. The bodies were then placed on one scaffold.

The relatives of the departed showed their grief by crying and wailing, giving away their possessions, and by giving a big feast for the others.

The people worshiped the Great Spirit and believed that when they died they would go to the Happy Hunting Ground. They believed the sun, water, land, eagles and coyotes were part of the Great Spirit. They knew the Great Spirit was good and wanted them to be good. They did not want to do anything that might displease the Great Spirit, such as killing an eagle and not begging its pardon and showing the proper reverence.

The medicine man was of good character. He had visions in which he could foretell the future. He interpreted dreams for the chief and others. He made medicines from roots and herbs for the sick. Visions told him what kind of charms to make and their uses. In order for his charms to work, he had to be kind, gentle, and good.

As the medicine man grew older, he chose his own successor. The successor had to be a young man above reproach and well liked by all the people. The young man told his dreams to the medicine man, and if the dreams were the right ones, the medicine man trained him to become his successor.

The people believed that the medicine man could cure them of sickness and wounds because he was good and lived according to the Great Spirit.

Before the Reservation: Chippewa Ways

Standing Chief

I never farmed.

Ouiskinawise and Shoshone, Chippewa from the country to the west of Lake Superior, were both born on the plains while their bands were on buffalo hunts in the early 1830s. In 1863 they had a son, Standing Chief, near Battle Creek in present-day Montana. His future wife, Clear Sky, was born at White Earth, Minnesota, in 1868 to Rising Sun and Love Thunder. Standing Chief provides detailed information on how the Chippewa did things: how they constructed wigwams, log cabins, and Red River carts; how they hunted buffalo and turned the animals into shelter, clothes, and food; how they traveled and forded streams and rivers. He answers the question: what was life like before the reservation?

WE USUALLY TRAVELED IN LARGE PARTIES, living in wigwams while we were traveling. Wigwams were made of buffalo hides. These hides were tanned; then a form was made of poles; the hides were stretched over this form and sewed to fit it. An opening was left on one side for a door, and at the top of the wigwam the hides were left loose so that an opening was made for the escape of the smoke. There was a flap left at the top that could be put down over the opening at night. In cold weather a fire was built in the center of the wigwam to keep us warm and also for cooking. The only furnishings in these wigwams were the buffalo robes which were used to sit on in the

Before the Reservation: Chippewa Ways

daytime and to sleep on at night. Sometimes we lived in these wigwams during the winter, but most of the time we would go to a camp along some creek or riverbank where there was plenty of timber. Here we usually built a log cabin for each family.

The logs were cut and hauled to the building site; the bark was taken off and the end of each log was notched; then the logs were placed one on top of the other until the desired height was reached. An opening was made for windows and a door. Buffalo hides were scraped until they were real thin, then tanned and stretched over the window openings. A buffalo hide was hung for the door. The cabin was usually about fourteen by fourteen feet in size. A fireplace was built at one end of the cabin for heating and cooking. This fireplace was made of poles and set out away from the wall and was built up to the roof. The inside of this frame was plastered with thick mud so that there would be no danger of it catching on fire. An opening was left at the top over the fireplace for the smoke to escape. The roof of the cabin was made of small poles placed close together with grass on top of the poles, then sod above that. The cracks in the walls were chinked with pieces of wood and then plastered both inside and out.

We usually made a wall of rocks around the cabins to keep the hostile Indians away and also to keep our horses from straying away. Sometimes the Sioux Indians would steal the horses.

In the spring when we started out on the hunt, we traveled with Red River carts in which the old men, women, and children rode. We had dogs also which were sometimes used to haul the little children, and the braves themselves usually rode on the ponies. We also used travois, made from poles, to carry their bedding and cooking utensils.

The Red River carts were made of wood. An ax was used to cut out the pieces for these carts. Any pieces that had to be shaped, such as the wheels, were cut and soaked in hot water until they could be bent into the shape desired, then tied with pieces of leather (thin strips called thongs cut for this use), then left to dry before using. Each cart had two wheels held together by a heavy piece of wood cut the width of the cart. A platform was made on this piece, and poles were fastened at each end of it to form the shafts. A rack of small poles was made on the platform. The old men, women, and children rode in this rack. We also used dogs

Standing Chief

Traveling by Red River Cart
The Red River carts continued to be used well into the 1900s.

for hauling purposes by fastening two light poles, one on each side of the dog, attached to a leather piece across the dog's chest. These poles extended far enough back of the dog to allow a basket made of buffalo hide to be fastened between them. The papoose or baby, or other small child, was sometimes placed in the basket to ride. Larger poles were used in the same way with ponies. The bedding, hides and tipis were tied to these poles far enough up from the end so as not to drag on the ground. Some of the men or older boys would ride these ponies to guide them but the dogs were left to travel by themselves.

Sometimes we would travel long distances before we would find a herd of buffalo. The braves rode a considerable distance ahead of the others, and when they sighted a herd, someone was sent back to tell the others to make camp. We would then halt, set up the wigwams, and unload the carts and travois. The children were then sent out to gather buffalo chips to use as fuel. In these camps the carts were placed in a circle to form a corral for the ponies at night. Early the following morning we would be up getting ready for the hunt. The old men, women, and children stayed in camp while the younger men went out on the hunt. When they saw the buffalo on the prairie, they would carefully work around them to get on the down-side of the wind, so that the buffalo

Before the Reservation: Chippewa Ways

would not smell them. Then they would race their horses toward the herd, each man picking out the buffalo he intended to kill. They would ride their horses right in among the buffalo, killing as many as they could. At first the Indians used bows and arrows, but the half-breeds used guns. They would sometimes chase the buffalo for miles, killing from five to ten each. Each had his arrow marked with a distinguishing mark, so that each family knew the buffalo that belonged to them.

As soon as a few buffalo had been killed, the women, old men, and the boys and girls who were old enough to help took the carts and went to get the meat. The animals were skinned where they had been killed, then cut up in pieces and hauled to camp. In the meantime the children had been very busy gathering buffalo chips. Long grass was also gathered and twisted into bundles to be used for burning while the meat was being dried into pemmican.

To make pemmican the meat was cut into long strips, one-half to one inch wide. These strips were then hung on a rack over a fire which smoked them and also dried them. The pieces were then laid on the flesh side of a buffalo hide, and beaten with sticks, one stick being used to hold the meat down and the other to beat it. This was continued until the meat was made tender by being cut into shreds. Some of the bones, especially the joints which contained much marrow, were cut or broken up as small as possible and placed in a large kettle, covered with water, and hung over a fire to boil. When these bones had cooked for a long time, they were taken out and the liquid set aside to cool. The fat which rose to the top and became hard was taken off and placed in a container to be used later. Meanwhile all of the flesh had been scraped off a buffalo hide, and the hide sewed up, forming a large sack. The thread used to sew the sack was made from the hide of the hump on the buffalo's shoulders. This hump was cut off, and all of the flesh scraped from it. This portion of hide was then placed near the fire to dry out. After it was well dried, it was separated into long pieces of thread — so to speak — actual name of these pieces being "thongs." This was very strong. After the sack was made, the fat with the meat which had been dried, smoked, and pounded into shreds, was placed in the sack, pounded down as it was put in, until it was filled. Sometimes dried berries were added for flavor.

Standing Chief

When the pemmican was wanted for use, it had to be cut out with a large knife, and sometimes it was so hard that an ax had to be used to loosen it.

To tan the buffalo hides for use, the hair was left on one side of those that were to be used as rugs and to be slept on, but for those that were to be used in making clothing, moccasins, and similar things the hair was removed before tanning. A frame was made of small poles; the hides were stretched on this frame and then scraped with a piece of flint until all the hair and flesh was off. The hide was then left in the frame until it was completely dried. It was then removed from the frame, and grease, which had been rendered from the fat of the buffalo, was rubbed on it, and a strong solution of soap and water was put on and left until the hide was thoroughly dampened. It was then rubbed until it was soft. Another frame or form was then made in the shape of a tipi. This was of light poles. The hide was wrapped around this, and a very slow fire was built of rotten wood under the hide, the smoke from which tanned the leather.

We used a type of rock called "flint" to build fires. We took dry twigs and leaves, put them in a pile, and rubbed two pieces of the flint together until sparks flew and set the pile on fire.

My father, Ouiskinawise, and our family were hunting in Canada when we saw our first train. We were in camp when an Indian on horseback came and told us he had seen a long black thing going swiftly across the prairie and that smoke was coming from it. We all watched for it and finally one day it came back. We did not know what it was. One day one of the Indian braves rode on the train, and when he came back, he told the others that it went so fast he "got there all at once."

One winter in about 1873 when I was ten years old, we were in camp near Chinook, Montana, and a white girl came there to teach us children. A log cabin had been built, and she taught school in this. In the morning she would go through the camp ringing a small bell. The children who wanted to attended, but none were compelled to go. We were taught our ABCs. This was all the school I ever attended.

When we traveled, we would ford the rivers we came to by fastening the carts together, one behind the other, in long lines. They were bound together with strong leather thongs. The tipis, buffalo robes, hides, and all other belongings were placed in the carts and securely fastened. The old men, women, and children rode in the carts. Some of the braves used long poles to guide the line (or raft) across the river. The braves and older boys rode the ponies, and the dogs had to swim across.

In the fall of 1877 father made camp for the winter near Glasgow, [Montana]. During the winter a general — an army man — came to talk with Chief Double Face, who was my grandfather. Then in the spring of 1878 we all were gathered up and taken to Fort Peck. We did not have to go as we had declared that we belonged in the United States. The Indians who belonged in Canada were sent back there, while those belonging on this side of the international boundary line were told to stay here.

After this we started on the way back east, hunting along the way as we went, but the buffalo were becoming very scarce and it was getting very hard for us to find means to live.

In 1880 I married a girl [Clear Sky] of the Chippewa tribe. We continued to live with my father.

In 1882 the family had only one pony and a colt left. We also had but one cart. At that time we were in the western part of Dakota Territory. We decided to move on to the Turtle Mountains. We loaded all that we could on the cart; the women carried the babies on their backs. We made packs of the rest of the belongings and carried these on our backs. We had to travel very slow on account of the children. We killed ducks, prairie chickens, and any other wild game we could find. We still had some pemmican and dried meat left. In the fall of 1882 we reached a place about two and one-half miles north of the present site of Dunseith, where we decided to make our home.

Father, my brother, and I cut logs and built a cabin about fourteen by fourteen. We made the roof of small poles, covered with grass which we cut in a slough, and lastly sod was placed on top of the grass. We used a white cloth sack for the window. The door was made of poles split and made into a sort of plank. A fireplace was built at one end of the house. There was no floor in the cabin. We did not have any furniture. We made our bed on the ground by spreading buffalo robes down and using some of the robes over them. In the daytime the robes were rolled up and used to sit on. We also built a small log barn for the pony and colt.

Standing Chief

We had a hard time living that winter. We hunted deer, elk, and rabbits and also trapped muskrats, weasels, and other fur-bearing animals.

In the spring of 1883 Chief Little Shell gave us a yoke of oxen, a wagon, and plow. I drove the oxen with a yoke and started to haul freight from Devils Lake, mostly salt pork. I traveled east until I came to a post office at Island Lake, where I stayed the first night. The rest of the way I went across the country, camping on the prairie at night. It took seven or eight days to make the trip.

In 1884, after the agency at Belcourt was started with Mr. Wells in charge, I hauled freight there. About this time I built a cabin for myself a few miles north of father's home.

After Dunseith was started, we trapped and traded furs at the stores there for groceries. I never farmed but did plant potatoes, corn, and other vegetables.

Chief Little Shell III
Little Shell argued that his people needed much more land than the two townships that the Turtle Mountain Reservation was reduced to in 1884 (SHSND B0307).

The Killing of Sitting Bull

Swift Hawk

Bullets, hatchets, knives were now flying through the air.

Swift Hawk was born in 1859 while his people were hunting in Montana. He was thirty-one years old when Sitting Bull was killed. Swift Hawk, who was a reservation policeman and was wounded in the action, presents his version of the events that surrounded Sitting Bull's death.

SITTING BULL AND HIS INDIANS WERE CAMPING by the Grand River about forty miles south of Fort Yates. The Indians were dancing day and night; little Indian children were dancing naked. They did not stop to eat.

Stories came in to Major McLaughlin [the agent] about what these Indians were doing. Most of these were exaggerated or untrue. McLaughlin sent Indian policemen out to Sitting Bull, telling him to stop the dancing. Sitting Bull sent back word that they were not doing any harm and would not stop. The other Sitting Bull Indians said if they tried to stop the dances, there would be trouble.

Major McLaughlin then decided to arrest Sitting Bull and bring him into the agency at Fort Yates. Thinking there might be trouble, he sent forty regular Indian policemen and eight or ten deputized Indians under command of Bullhead. Soldiers were to follow shortly afterward and would be there in case of trouble.

Swift Hawk

Indian Policemen from Standing Rock Reservation
Photographed in a studio at Fort Yates (SHSND Fiske 0305).

Most of the Indian policemen did not think there was going to be any trouble and some of them had little ammunition. Most had rifles and some revolvers. We left Fort Yates on horseback on December 14, 1890. That night we camped on the Grand River a few miles away from Sitting Bull's camp.

We arrived in Sitting Bull's camp about four in the morning. It was dark and a cold rain was falling. Some went up to Sitting Bull's log house. Bull Head, Shave Head, Weasel Bear, Red Tomahawk, Eagle Man, and Brave Bear went in. Brown Dog, Not Afraid of Anything, Afraid of Hawk, Little Soldier, and I went in Sitting Bull's other log house to look for guns. The other policemen were scattered around the two log houses.

Bull Head told Sitting Bull he would have to go to Fort Yates. Sitting Bull said he would not go and that they would have to kill him first. They grabbed him and took him out the door; just then some of Sitting Bull's Indians came running up; one of them saw the policeman had Sitting Bull; he raised his gun, fired, and the fight started. Bullhead shot Sitting Bull and then fell, mortally wounded himself. Shave Head

The Killing of Sitting Bull

coming out the door was shot through the stomach; he had his hands down holding his intestines in. Bullets, hatchets, knives were now flying through the air. I and the others came out of the other cabin just as this happened. We joined in the fight; everyone was yelling and shooting and some crying. Shortly after the fight started I was struck by a bullet, just grazing my head; I fell down and was trampled by the other Indians. Some of the policemen ran into Sitting Bull's house. They pulled out Sitting Bull's boy and killed him. I came to before the fight was over and managed to crawl over and get Bullhead's rifle and take a few more shots. Most of the policemen managed to get in the log houses. Some of the policemen during the fight fell or were knocked down.

The fight lasted until the sun came up, and shortly after that we heard a bugle blowing; some shots were fired toward the cabins of Sitting Bull. Red Tomahawk put a white rag on a stick and went to meet the soldiers and let them know the fight was over. They then loaded up the dead and wounded and took them to Fort Yates. Bullhead and Shave Head died shortly after. The Indian policemen were kept in their quarters and no one was allowed to see them. They were all questioned in regard to the fight. Feelings ran very high, and many Indians were very angry with the policemen. Policemen had to be very careful for many years after this as many of the Indians held this fight against them.

I and the other policemen were taken and put in jail at Fort Rice where we were questioned by the army officers. We were questioned separately and did not know the others were there. I was questioned different times for two days and then sent back to Fort Yates. The rest were sent back shortly also.

These stories about the policemen being drunk are untrue, and they were just started to put the blame on the policemen. Red Tomahawk left Fort Yates after the other policemen had started. He joined them in the camp on Grand River before the fight. Major McLaughlin gave him pieces of white cloth, so that each man could tie one around his neck and there would not be any mistake in the dark as to who were policemen.

Two Bulls

Fighting Custer, Fleeing to Canada

Two Bulls

I took part in the charge against Custer. His horse was shot from under him.

About 1850 Two Bulls was born in the woodlands of Minnesota where he spent his boyhood. When he was ten years old, his camp moved westward across the plains and the Missouri River. For the next sixteen years he spent most of his time on the hunt as his camp moved from place to place in present-day western North Dakota and eastern Montana. He presents a unique account of his participation in the Battle of the Little Big Horn and life in Canada after the battle.

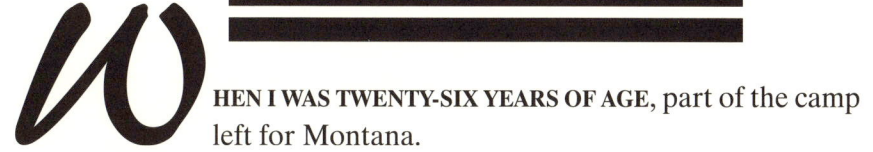

WHEN I WAS TWENTY-SIX YEARS OF AGE, part of the camp left for Montana.

At this time the government was having trouble with the Indians and wanted the Indians to come in and make a new treaty in regard to reservation boundaries. The white people were going into the Black Hills, and the soldiers could not keep them out.

At the time we left for Montana, we heard of the proclamation of the War Department that any Indians not on the reservation by a certain date would be called hostile Indians and that the soldiers were coming to bring them back. As this was wintertime, we could not get back, and most of us did not want to go back anyway.

77

Fighting Custer, Fleeing to Canada

Sitting Bull and Crazy Horse at the Little Big Horn
Pictograph by Sioux artist Amos Bad Heart Bull

In the early spring of the year we were camping in the Wolf Mountains on the Rosebud Creek. Many bands of Sioux were here. They had many scouts out in the hills, watching for the soldiers. One day scouts brought back the report that many soldiers were coming. The young warriors all went out on horseback. Most of us had Winchester rifles. That night when it got dark, we stopped and camped. In the morning we started out again and soon ran into the army scouts. These scouts were Indians from enemy tribes — Crows, Arapahoes, and Blackfeet — and we enjoyed this fight much better than fighting the soldiers. When this fight started, some of the army scouts rode back and told the soldiers. They came up as quickly as they could. We forced the soldiers to retreat. The fight lasted from early morning until late in the afternoon. The soldiers retreated, and the last I saw of them, they had stopped to camp. This gave our camp a chance to move on up into the mountains. Later we joined the other Sioux Indians on the Little Big Horn.

In camp on the Little Big Horn were thousands of Sioux Indians. They spent their time having powwows. They knew the soldiers were coming and had many scouts out in the hills. Many of these Indians knew General Custer.

On June 25, 1876, the camp was attacked by Reno from the north and Custer from the south. I was with the Indians that attacked Reno. Some of us turned back and were in time to help surround General Custer. I took part in the charge against him. His horse was shot from under him. The fight did not last long. After this, some of us went back to fight Reno again. We could not drive the soldiers out.

After the Custer fight, I and the band I was in roamed around in the Rosebud country and in the Wolf Mountains where we spent the

Two Bulls

winter. Game was scarce, and we had a very hard time to keep from starving. In the month of March, called "Sore Eyes" month, we joined a band of Yankton Indians who had not taken part in the Custer fight.

Many of the Indians had moved into Canada, where they had freedom and were not molested by soldiers. I and my band also decided to move into Canada where we would not be bothered by the soldiers. So after being with the Yankton Indians about a month, we moved northward. Game became more plentiful as we moved on, and we felt better.

The strip of land that formed the border between the United States and Canada was called by the Indians "Holy Line," and we knew we could live in peace north of this line. As we neared the border, it was reported that soldiers were coming behind us. We hurried to cross the line. We saw the rocks that marked the border, and we knew that we were safe. We traveled for ten days into Canada and joined the other Sioux Indians. We went through one large town that we called "Red Coat Town" because there were many soldiers with red coats.

We joined the other Sioux in the Wood Mountains. Many of these Sioux there had no part in the Custer fight; they had come before the fight. I spent four years in Canada. The government of Canada did not bother us. We were free, and we liked it there. We made our living hunting and trapping. There were plenty of buffalo; we ate the meat and sold the hides. In the winter, we trapped all kinds of fur-bearing animals, which we traded with the fur companies. We were well treated in Canada, and we liked it very much.

Catholic priests came to us and told us in conferences that the U.S. government wanted us to come back to Standing Rock Reservation to live. They promised us that the government would feed and take care of us. The priests agreed to help us also, and many of us Indians became Catholics.

I and many of the Indians decided to leave Canada. We came down to Fort Peck about 1880. We lived around Fort Peck and Miles City until 1882 when we were brought down the river in a steamer to Fort Yates on the Standing Rock Reservation.

Childhood, Marriage, A Deadly Fire, and an Eclipse of the Sun

Childhood, Marriage, A Deadly Fire, and an Eclipse of the Sun

Pretty Shawl

Our people thought the sun was dying and were very badly frightened.

> Pretty Shawl's Lakota people were camped near present-day Gettysburg, South Dakota, when she was born about 1860. Her father was Chief Two Bears, and her mother was one of his wives. Her family reflected traditional Lakota ways prior to its move to the Standing Rock Reservation. Her story reveals a great deal about her tribe and its ways.

THERE WERE THREE RINGS OF TIPIS in our camp that probably numbered about 1,500 people. Two Bears was chief of our tribe. He was a good chief and a friend of the white people.

My mother was the youngest of four sisters. My name was Pretty Shawl before I was married. As a little girl I played with the other children, made dolls and little bags, sewed for my mother, carried water and sticks, picked wild fruit and vegetables. We made our clothing of tanned hides and some cotton goods. A few white traders would come to camp and trade cloth for hides and furs.

Pretty Shawl

Oglala Sioux Perform a Dance with Horses
Pictograph by Kills Two, Sioux artist.

    As a little girl I was afraid of the medicine men. I did not like to go to the ceremonies when the medicine men were dressed in bearskins and buffalo robes. I was also afraid of the enemy tribes who sometimes attacked the camp at night. Most of the time we had scouts out, so the enemy could not surprise us. If a scout saw any of the enemy, he would return and notify the camp. The women, children, and old men were given horses so they could leave the camp in case of battle. After one of these fights we would move to a new camping ground. The women packed everything and tied the bundles and babies on a travois. The men then brought up the horses and tied the travois to them. The women led the horses, and most of the time they had to walk while the men rode. An announcer came around and told us what to do and when to move.

    I had eleven brothers, who were all good hunters, so we always had plenty of meat to eat. My brothers often went on the warpath and raided many enemy camps. They managed to get many horses in this way. Before the men left camp, they usually had a war dance, and when they came back with scalps and horses, they would have a victory dance. They blackened their faces for this dance. Three of my brothers were killed in these raids. Anyone who died was wrapped in shawls or blankets and hides and then tied on a scaffold placed on four poles. Every time someone died, the camp was moved.

I was married four times. We did not have any marriage ceremony. If a man and woman liked each other, they went to live in one of their parent's tipis, or the man would be given a tipi of his own by his parents. If they did not get along, they separated and lived with someone else. When they separated, the children were left to be taken care of by the grandparents.

One time when I was a little girl, there was an eclipse of the sun; our people thought the sun was dying and were very badly frightened.

Chief Two Bears, Pretty Shawl's Father (SHSND 0004-024)

Once we had just moved camp and had our tipis put up when we saw a large prairie fire coming. We took pails and threw water from a nearby creek on the tipis. We tried to get the horses together and drive them across the creek but could not get them all. Children were also taken across the creek. When the fire came through the camp, many babies and some of the older people were killed. Some of the tipis were burned down, and many horses died.

When Fort Rice was built we spent three winters near there.

Index

Arapahoe, 78

Arikara (Sanish), 29, 55

Assiniboine, 24

Belcourt (ND), 33, 34, 35, 73

Bismarck (ND), 37, 38

Blackfeet, 23, 29, 49-50, 78

Buffalo hunting and uses of, 4-5, 8, 11-12, 20-23, 24-26, 27-28, 31-33, 36, 43, 45-46, 48-49, 54, 58, 62, 69-71

Cannon Ball, including agency, 3, 12, 26, 40, 41, 46, 47

Childhood, 1, 7-8, 27-28, 29-30, 40, 46-47, 48, 55-56, 58, 62, 80-82

Chippewa, 20-26, 31-38, 42-44, 51-54, 67-73

Clothing, 8, 54, 80

Cree, 24, 32

Crow, 2, 5-6, 27-28, 29, 43, 49, 78

Custer, Col. George Armstrong, 77-79

Death and burial, 16, 30, 32, 27, 65-66, 81-82

Devils Lake, 16, 18, 20, 33, 36

Dunseith (ND), 52, 72

Eagles, 57, 63-64

Farming, 34, 44, 47, 51-54, 73

Food (other than buffalo), 2, 8, 9, 14, 39, 40, 49, 53

Fort Abercrombie, 23, 24

Fort Assiniboine, 25

Fort Berthold, 24

Fort Buford, 57

Fort Totten, 13-19, 24, 35

Fort Wadsworth, 23

Fort Yates, 2, 8, 9, 30, 46, 47, 61, 62, 74, 75, 76, 79

Freight hauling, 15, 16, 33, 35, 36, 73

Games, 2, 18

Government, tribal, 62-68

Guiding, 23-24

Hampton Institute, 62

Health, 2, 8, 30, 40, 47

Hidatsa, 23, 24, 55, 57, 58-60

Horse raids and inter-tribal conflict, 2, 5-6, 23, 30, 46-48, 50, 54, 47, 58, 68, 81

Housing (tipi, wigwam, log), 8, 9, 33, 35, 44, 46, 63, 67-68, 72-73

Indian police, 2-3, 9-10, 61, 74-76

83

Index

Lakota, 1-3, 4-6, 7-12, 27-28, 29-30, 48-50, 61-66, 74-76, 77-79, 80-82

Little Big Horn, battle of, 77-79

Little Shell, 34, 44, 83

McLaughlin, Major James, 19, 61, 74

Mandan, 55-58

Marriage, 40, 65, 82

Pawnee, 49

Pembina (ND), 51

Porcupine Substation, 61

Ranching, 3, 12, 47

Red River cart, 31, 52, 54, 68-69

Red Thunder, 26

Riel, Louis, 25, 44

Sacagawea, 13

Schooling, 9-10, 31, 34, 36-37, 40, 54, 62, 71-72

Sitting Bull, 1-3, 12, 17, 25, 44, 61, 74-76

Smallpox, 17, 58-59

Snake root, 37

Spirituality, including Sun Dance, 35, 37, 39-41, 43, 56-57, 58, 59, 60, 66

Standing Rock Reservation, 40, 46

Trapping, 2, 25, 63-64, 73

Turtle Mountains (including reservation), 25, 26, 33, 34, 37, 44, 52, 72

United States Army, 16, 18-19, 72, 77-79

Yankton, 45-47, 79

Yanktonai, 39-41, 45-47, 79

About the editors . . .

      Historian D. Jerome Tweton returned to his hometown, Grand Forks, North Dakota, to teach in the University of North Dakota history department in 1965 after receiving his Ph.D. from the University of Oklahoma. For most of his thirty-year tenure at the University, he served as department chairman. Tweton's books include The Marquis de Morès: Dakota Capitalist, French Nationalist *and* The New Deal at the Grassroots: Programs for the People in Otter Tail County, Minnesota. *A senior consultant to the North Dakota state partner of the National Endowment for the Humanities, Tweton has written and edited books and articles about the history of North Dakota for citizens of all ages, including text books and instructional material for classroom use. In addition to his work as an academic historian who has edited publications, written seven books and scores of articles, Tweton has participated in over 300 public humanities programs in North Dakota and throughout the nation. He and his wife Paula own and operate a bed-and-breakfast in a renovated turn-of-the-century home which is on the National Register of Historic Places, the Beiseker Mansion in Fessenden, North Dakota.*

      Everett C. Albers has served as the executive director of The North Dakota Humanities Council, the state partner of the National Endowment for the Humanities, since it began in 1973. Albers is one of the founders of the modern Chautauqua movement which features first-person characterizations of historical writers and thinkers presented in tents during summer tours of the Great Plains. He holds an M.A. in English from Colorado State University and has taught humanities and English. A North Dakota native who grew up on a family homestead in Oliver County, Albers lives with his wife Leslie in Bismarck. They are the parents of Albert and Gretchen. Albers operates Otto Design, a desktop publishing concern, as an avocation. He co-edited The Legacy of North Dakota Country Schools *and the 1998* Behold Our New Century: Early 20th Century Visions of America *and has written several children's coloring books featuring Seaman, the dog who went with Lewis and Clark.*